Contents:

Chapter 1
Brief history of marbling

Marbling is an ancient craft. It originated in Japan. Suminagashi translated is literally 'floating ink'. Initially only black ink was used and much later other colours were introduced. The technique involved touching a water surface with ink then turpentine. The first examples of suminagashi were found around the 12th century. Papers were used by nobility.

There is evidence of marbling in Turkey, Persia, China and India during the 15th century. It is possible that suminagashi travelled to the other parts of the world via the Silk Route.

In Turkey marbling is called 'Ebru' meaning 'clouds'. It was developed there in the 17th century. Ebru marbling is similar to the marbling we achieve; the design is created as the focal point of the print and not only used as a background. Ebru marbling includes the use of a size or thickened water on which the paints float, otherwise pigments are too heavy and will simply fall through water.

It is thought that marbling was brought to Europe by Venetian merchants around the 16th and 17th centuries. Marbling was introduced to Italy, then France, Germany, Spain, Holland, Britain and other western countries.

By the 17th century marbling techniques had been developed further in France, Germany and Holland. It was only by the end of the 17th to the beginning of the 18th century, that marbling papers were being produced in England. By the mid 18th century, English papers had improved to the standard produced by other European countries.

As marbling was developed in different countries, techniques were given names, i.e. Spanish Moire, Dutch, French curl, etc.

Chapter 2

Contents of the current full marbling kit

In your kit you have:

1. Two trays.

The lid is one tray and the base can be used as another.

2. Six pots of concentrated paint.

Three primary colours (red, yellow and blue), black, white and violet. These colours can be mixed into other colours. A more in depth description of colour mixing can be found on p. 7.

3. Eight pipettes.

These are to drop paint onto the water surface. They have other uses as well: They enable you to draw up paint from paint pots, draw up water for dilution before marbling (as described on p. 6) and can be used as a cleaner if drops fall through the floater to the bottom of the tray. There are more pipettes than number of paints. This will give you the opportunity to mix and use other colours like orange and green.

4. Alum (alum potash).

This is used as a mordant. That is a preparation for some marbling surfaces. Instructions for using alum are on p. 4 and 9.

5. Floater powder.

This is a thickening agent. It is also called the size. Once mixed into the soft water and cooled, it is poured into the tray. The paint is dropped onto the floater. Instructions for mixing the floater are included in the kit and also on p. 4. For the duration of the book, the size will be referred to as the floater. Your floater powder is derived from plants. Over a period of between 3 weeks to 3 months if kept in the fridge, it will lose its viscosity and will become more watery. You may discard the thin batch down the sink as it is non-toxic.

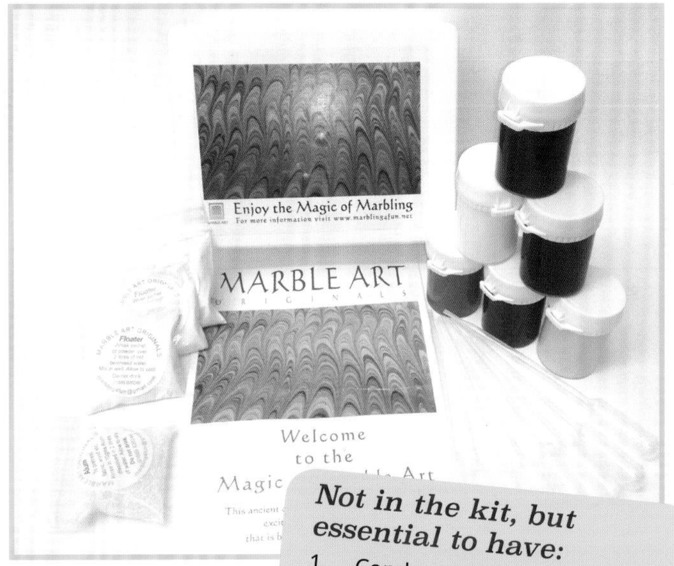

Not in the kit, but essential to have:

1. Combs of different widths.
2. A stylus (straightened paper clip or cocktail stick).
3. Items to marble onto. (See chapter 5).

Not in the kit, but handy to use:

1. Clothes you don't mind to get stained in case paint drops on you.
2. Plastic sheeting to protect the table used for marbling, i.e. a bin liner.
3. Air tight containers for diluted paint.
4. Any size tray of at least 2.5cm deep can be used.
5. Kitchen roll for cleaning after each print.

Chapter 3
Preparations before marbling

1. Preparing alum

Dilute 10g of alum per 2 litres of water (or alternatively 5g/ litre).

Dissolve the alum in hot water.

Storage:
Store in a clean, plastic container with lid.
Label 'alum' and do not drink.

This type of alum is non-toxic, but extremely unpleasant to taste. Keep in a cool place and out of reach of children and animals.

It can be used for up to three months after being dissolved.

If the alum is to be used for items that do not include fabric, you can mix the alum (using the above ratios) and pour it into a spray bottle. Items can then be sprayed and left to dry before marbling. (See chapter 5).

2. Prepare your floater.

See label on floater powder for information on how much water: floater powder is needed. Pour the right quantity of soft water in a saucepan.

Heat this water on a cooker or kettle to just below boiling point.

Weigh out the correct ratio of floater powder as indicated in the kit.

Turn off the heat. Safety comes first. Remember that you are working with hot water. Take care.

Sprinkle the floater powder onto the surface of the hot water while whisking. This ensures the floater is evenly distributed without forming blobs.

Leave to stand for 12 hours or over night.

Pour back into a clean, detergent free container.

The floater is now ready to use.

Storage:
Keep in a clean container.

Label the container: "Floater, do not drink" with a date on which the floater was made. Store in a cold place, i.e. your fridge.

If it was kept in a fridge, leave it to become room temperature before use.

Mixing your floater - water issues

A note on water for floater mixing:

For best printing results *use soft water*. Hard water will either make paint drop through the floater, will spread too quickly, bead quickly and it will be much harder to obtain patterns. The print will be of much poorer quality.

Soft water can easily be obtained. Battery top up water, deionised or distilled water is recommended. (It has a water hardness of <10 mg/l) It can either be found in the ironing or hardware sections of most supermarkets. Condensed water from tumble dryer or air conditioning units is also good- and free.

You may be lucky enough to live in a soft water area. See map for an approximate indication of the water hardness of your area.

! Top Tips (The limescale in your kettle may be a good indication of the hardness of the water in your area: No or very little limescale means that you probably have soft water). A water hardness test kit is a better indication of your water hardness. *Note that water hardness can change daily.*

Always mix more floater than the capacity of the tray you are going to use. This will enable you to top up the tray after some prints have been completed. For example, mix 2 litres if the tray being used has a capacity of one litre.

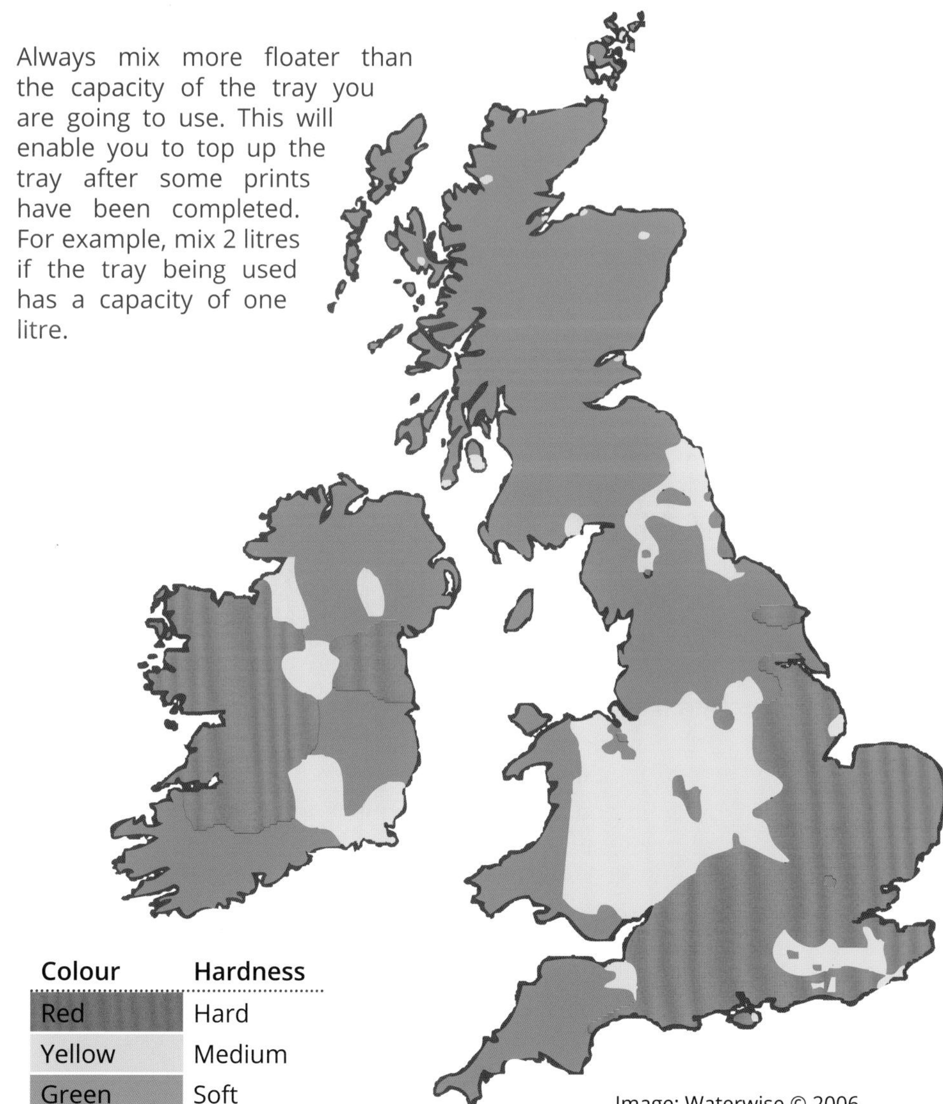

Image: Waterwise © 2006

Chapter 4
Preparations on the day of marbling

1. Prepare a surface like a table which you can use for all your equipment. It may be more comfortable to sit, so have a chair ready.
2. Protect the table with a waterproof material, for example plastic sheeting obtainable at most hardware stores or a bin liner.
3. If your floater was kept in a cool place, allow it to return to room temperature.
4. Wear clothing that you don't mind getting stained in case any of the paint drop on you.
5. Open your kit, remove the lid if you choose to use the lid of the starter kit as a tray for floating the paint onto. Remember that any size tray can be used, as long as it is a minimum of 2.5 cm or 1 inch deep.
6. Fill the tray to the brim with your floater liquid.
7. Now for diluting your paints:
   a) Use any suitable container to house the paints. We use air tight containers which are obtainable at www.marbling4fun.net.
   b) The marbling paints need to be diluted 1:1 with soft water.
   c) Use a pipette:
      i. Draw up one measure of the soft water. Release this into the empty container.
      ii. Draw up one measure of the paint and release this into the soft water. (If more paint is needed for the day's marbling, use more measures of water: paint).
      iii. Mix the paint and soft water thoroughly by drawing up the mixture into the pipette and releasing it back into the contain. Do this several times until you are confident that the paint and water have mixed.
8. Mix all the colours you would like to use.
9. Have the items to be marbled at hand.

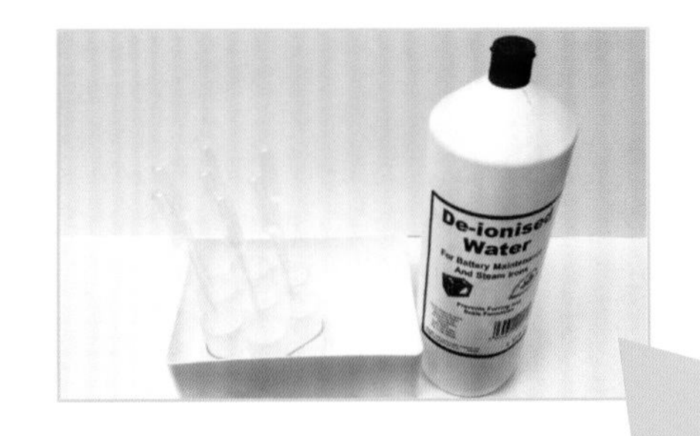

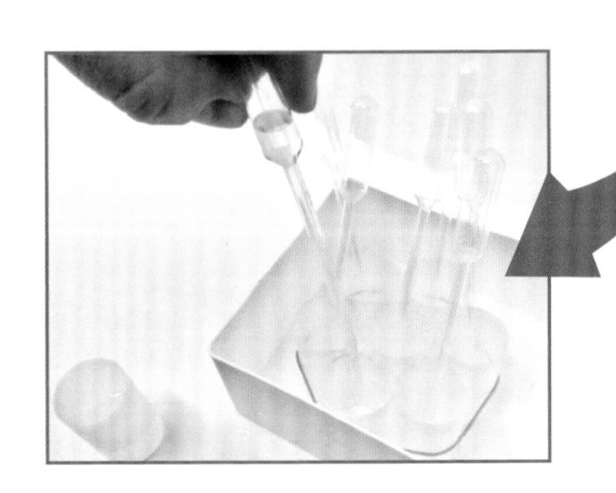

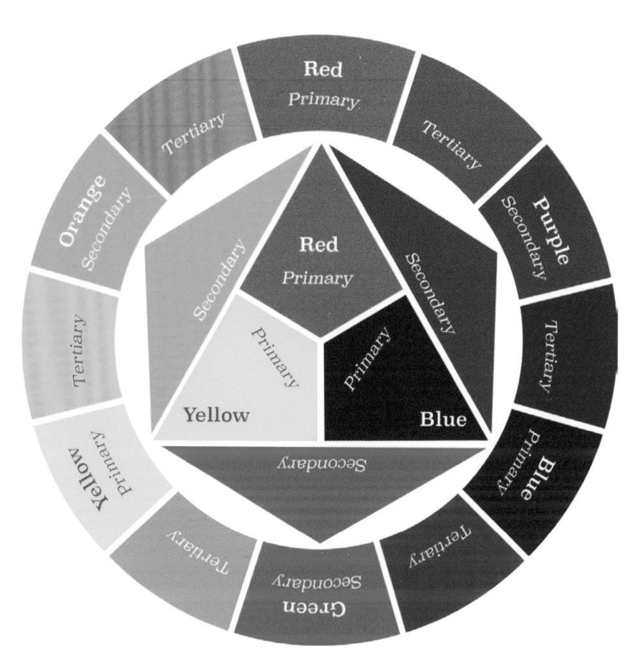

For example:

Two primary colours mix into a secondary:
Yellow+red=orange.

A secondary with a primary (next to it), makes a tertiary colour:
Orange+red=Dark orange
Orange+yellow=Light orange

Blue+yellow=Green (Secondary)
Green+ Blue=Dark green(Tertiary)
Green+Yellow=Lime green(Tertiary)

Blue+Red=Purple(Secondary)
Purple+Blue=Indigo(Tertiary)
Purple+Red=Violet(Tertiary)

Mixing your colours:

Start with the lightest primary colour first. Add one drop at a time of the darker primary until you have the colour you would like.

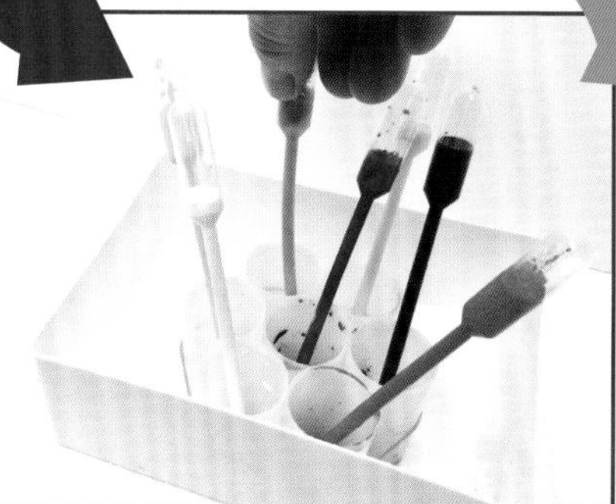

Chapter 5
Choosing, preparing & marbling objects

Paper

Choosing paper

Most papers marble well. The greater wet strength paper has, the heavier the paper the more paint it can absorb. Paper is measured in grams per square meter. The heavier, the paper, the more paint it can absorb. We have found that 160g photocopying paper works well.

Paper that won't work well:

- Paper with a glossy or plastic finish.
- Too thin paper that does not have a good wet strength.

Marbling paper:

a) Cut to size- just smaller than the tray you are using.

b) Slightly curl the paper before rolling it onto the paint. (This is to avoid air pockets being trapped which will result in a white circle).

c) Lift off straight away.

d) If alum was used or there is excess paint on the print:

e) Spray paper gently with water once lifted off.

f) Leave to drip dry.

1. cut and fold paper

Preparing paper

Paper does not have to be alumed, but you may if you would like to.

a) Dip a sponge into the alum solution.

b) Wipe over the paper surface.

c) Allow to dry naturally.

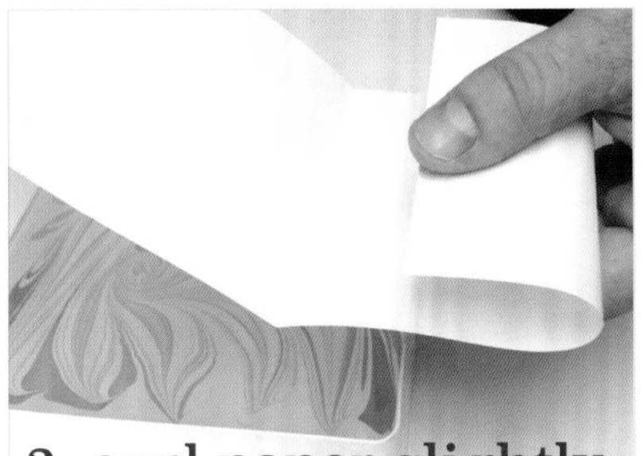

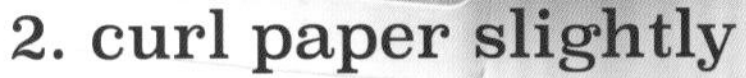

2. curl paper slightly

3. gently roll onto paint in one movement...

4. ...until flat

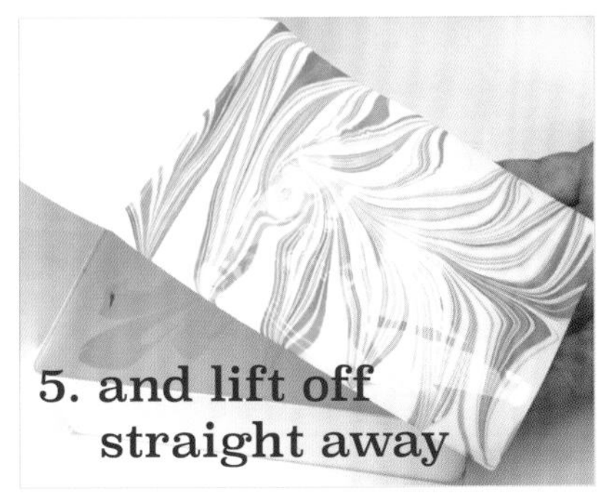

5. and lift off straight away

Pottery

Pottery doesn't need to be alumed.

a) Pottery has to be bisque. It cannot be glazed or varnished. (The paint needs a natural fibre to stain.)

b) Whatever you choose, must have a flat or slightly curved surface. This will avoid air bubbles. The paint will avoid air pockets.

Leather

1. Tooling leather is best to use.
2. Light leather will allow the marbling colours to show up.
3. Spray the leather using the spray bottle.
4. Or dip a sponge in the alum solution and wipe over the leather.
5. Leave to dry naturally.

Cork

a) The lighter the cork, the more colours of the paint will show through.

b) Once you have chosen what cork you would like to use, dip it in the alum solution.

c) Or spray the cork with the alum solution using a spray bottle.

d) Leave to dry naturally.

Wood

Choosing wood:

a) Raw, unvarnished wood has to be chosen.

b) It should not have a protective layer.

c) Decide what effect you would like. The lighter the wood, the more of the marbling colour will show.

d) Smooth wood, free of dust and grease is needed.

e) Remember the marbling inks are transparent, so any markings, colour and character of the wood will show through.

Preparing wood:

a) Briefly dip the wood in an alum solution for no longer than 10 seconds.

b) Leave to dry.

c) Alternatively, use the spray bottle and spray the wood. (As described on p.4)

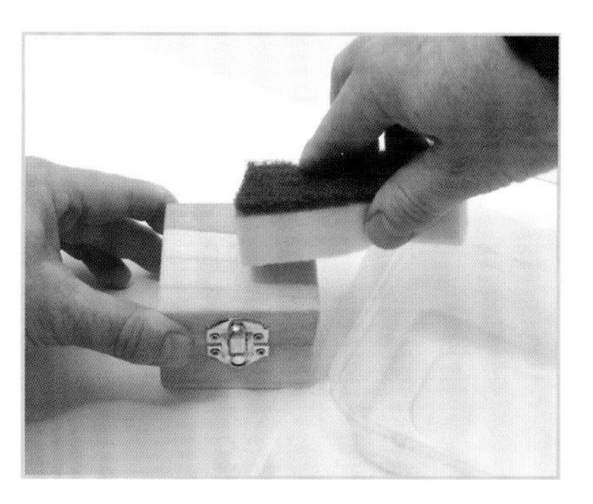

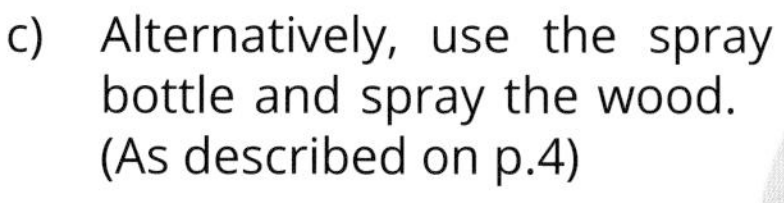

Chapter 5
Choosing, preparing & marbling objects

Choosing and preparing the best fabric to marble onto:

The paint was developed to use on natural fibres. However, we have found that some synthetic or fabric mixes achieve similar results than some natural fibres. Fabrics that are good to use are: cotton, viscose, linen, calico, muslin, silk, satin.

Testing Fabric

a) Take a little pot of water to the fabric shop. (Ask permission before testing). Most shop keepers do not mind if you explain why you need to test the fabric.

b) Take a tiny corner of the chosen fabric. Dip it into the water.

c) If the fabric absorbs the water fast, it should also absorb the marbling paint well and offer good marbling results.

d) If the fabric repels the water, the fabric will also not absorb the paint well. Therefore that fabric will not offer the best results.

Preparing Fabric

a) Wash the fabric in water only to get rid of any chemicals used in the production.

b) Submerge fabric in alum solution.

c) Leave the fabric for 3 minutes in the solution.

d) Drip dry the fabric.

e) Cut fabric slightly larger than the tray you are using for marbling.

lay fabric onto the tray

The fabric we use works exceptionally well and is available on www.marbling4fun.net

Press corners of fabric firmly into container. When the design shows through, lift the fabric off the floater.

Chapter 6
Basic technique

> If I was allowed to give only one piece of information it would be this:
> **be gentle with the pipette. Gently pinch, never squeeze.**

Follow similar principles for all the items to be marbled.

a) A tray of at least 2.5cm need to be filled with floater liquid. (Before pouring the floater, tilt the bottle to maintain even mixing, but do not shake).

b) Cover the surface with a background colour: *These drops are released in close succession randomly over the floater surface.*

   i) Keep the diluted paint stirred by pinching and releasing the pipette.

   ii) Draw up paint in the pipette.

   iii) Keep the pipette about 1cm from the floater surface.

   iv) Very gently pinch the pipette.

   v) Wait for the drops to open up.

c) Add colours for the design, one drop at a time.

d) Create the design with either a stylus (cocktail stick or straightened paper clip) or comb.

e) Print.

f) Leave the design to dry.

Cleaning tools and tray when finished:

a) Rinse using water. (We don't use chemicals as any residue will react with the paint during your future marbling sessions.)

b) If some paint has dried and more stubborn, use a scourer.

c) Store for your next session.

There are slight differences between marbling fabric and paper:

Marbling fabric:

a) Use as much paint to cover the surface of the floater. Stop when the paint slowly opens.

b) When printing: Keep the fabric taut and lay it down flat onto the paint.

c) Push your fingers into the corners for the print to reach all the areas of the fabric.

d) Gently rinse in water before drying.

Marbling paper:

a) Use about 8 drops of paint for the background colour.

b) When printing: Slightly curl the paper which is about to be printed. This avoids air pockets.

c) Lower the paper in one continuous movement (apart from the Spanish design described page 32)

A Selection of Tools

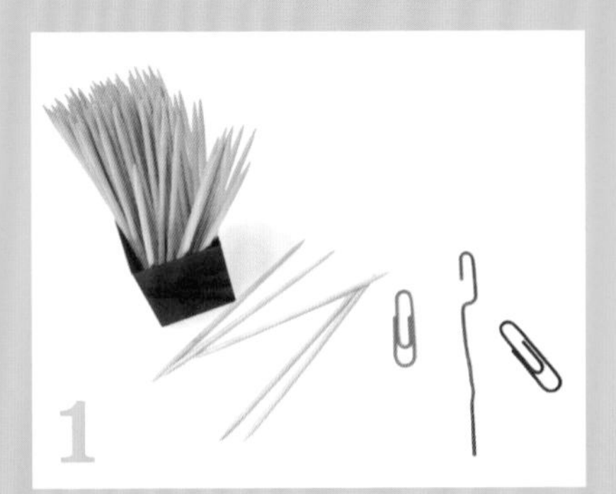

A stylus:
It can be either a straightened paper clip
Or a cocktail stick.

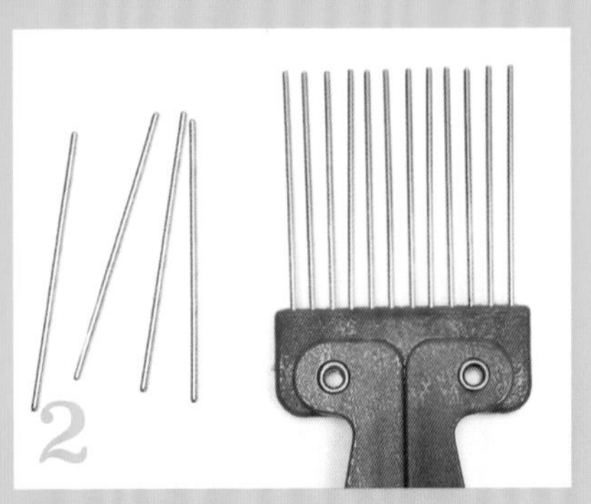

A comb:
No teeth removed. For the nonpareil design. A home made comb can also work well.
(See p.29)

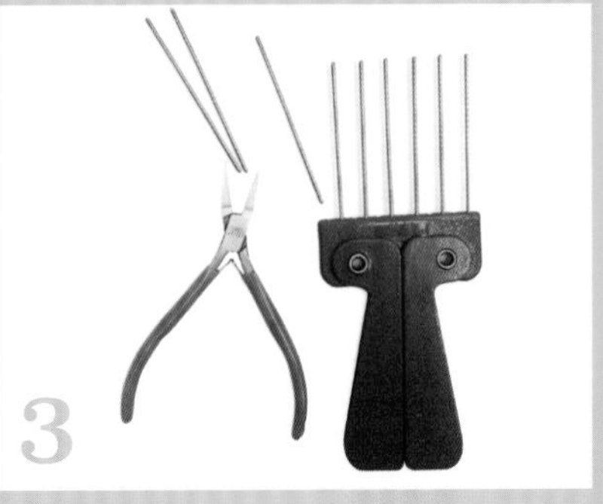

A comb:
Every second tooth removed which offers a larger rake.

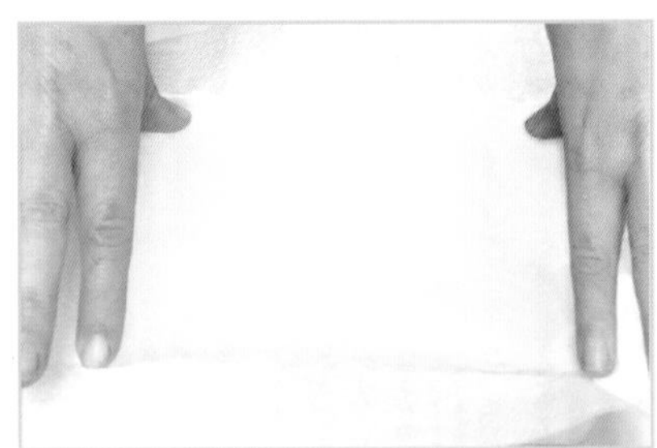

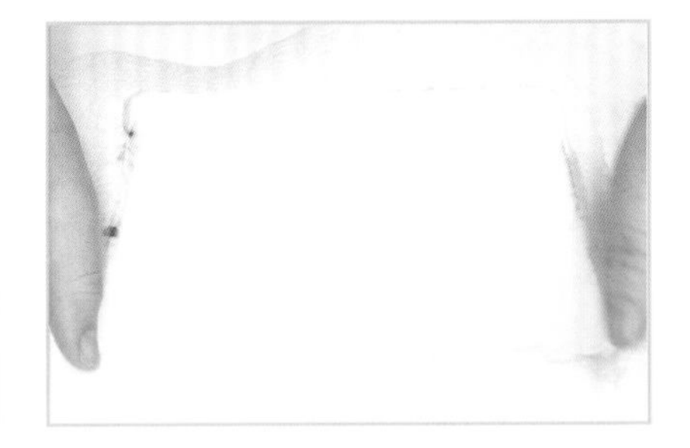

Start each new design with a clean floater surface!

Cleaning after each print:

- Not every print will clean the floater surface, especially when printing paper.
- Whatever paint is left from the first print, can be changed into another design, and a lighter print will be obtained.
- It is possible to achieve a third print. The 'Ghost design' is obtained when the design is left and printed as it is.
- If there is still any paint left, clean using either kitchen towel or scrap paper.

Start marbling!

Here is a selection of some of the designs in the book which turned into a small wall hanging.

I am not a quilter-yet. Perhaps one day the blocks will align perfectly to the millimetre. Perhaps. It would be nice. Even better than perfection is the thorough enjoyment of marbling and the making of something with the prints: A patchwork quilt or cushion, a purse or bag.

Neither am I a bookbinder- not yet anyway. Perhaps one day leather bound books with stunning marbled endpapers will be made. Perhaps. That would be some achievement. Till then I will happily sew three hole saddle stitched books or perhaps create hardcovers, using marbled fabric for cloth.

Whether you are a professional quilter, bookbinder, card maker, crafter or a person who would like to explore the beautiful craft of marbling, enjoy the journey to creating unique pieces of artwork.

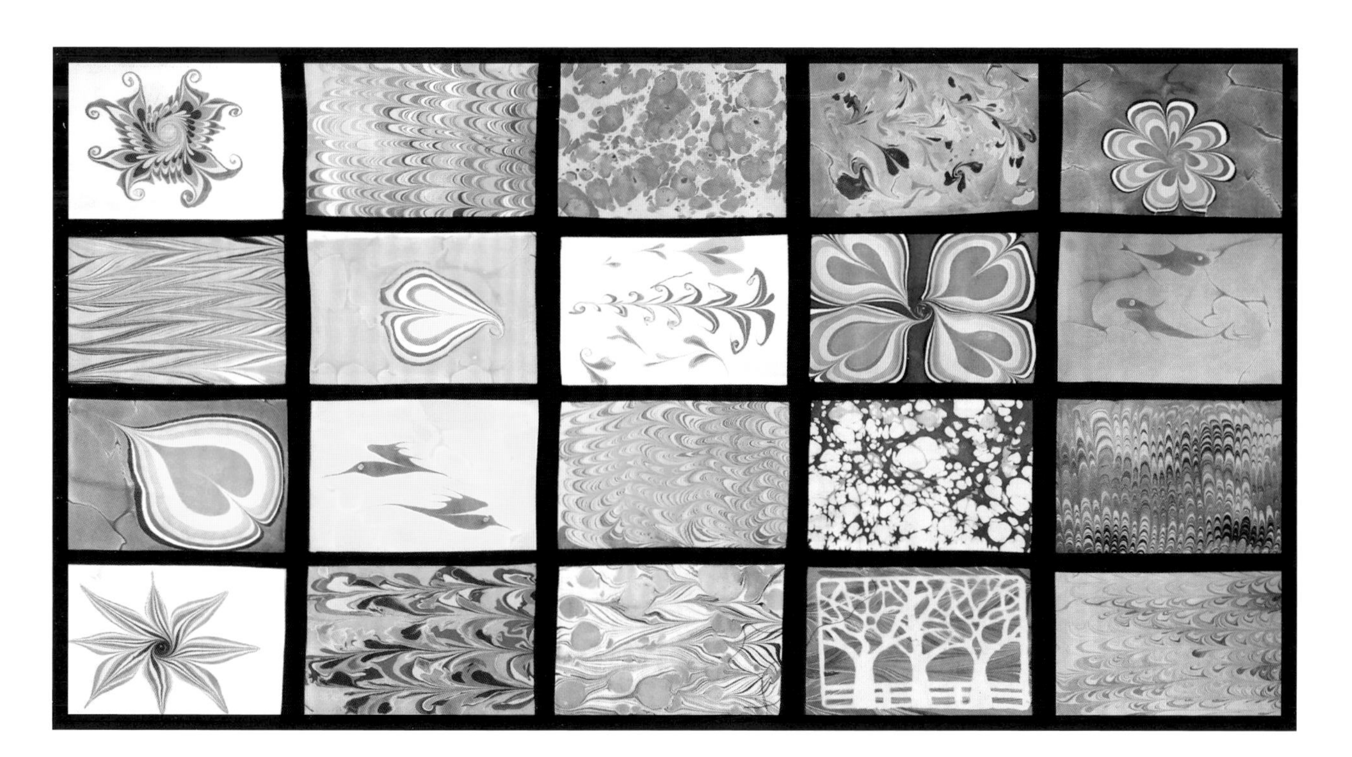

Chapter 6: Contemporary designs
Flower design

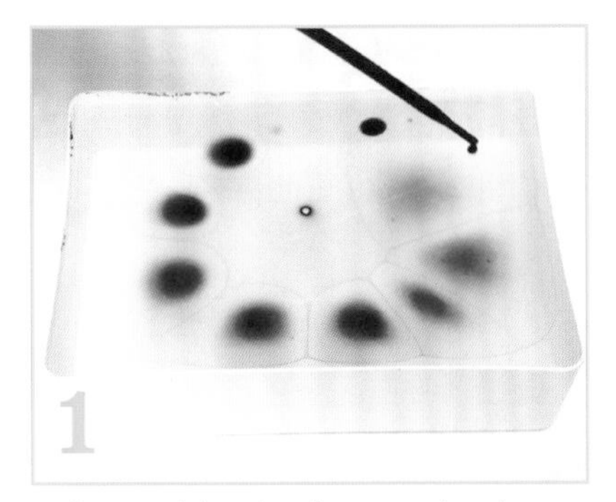

Start with a background colour. Wait for the drops to open up.

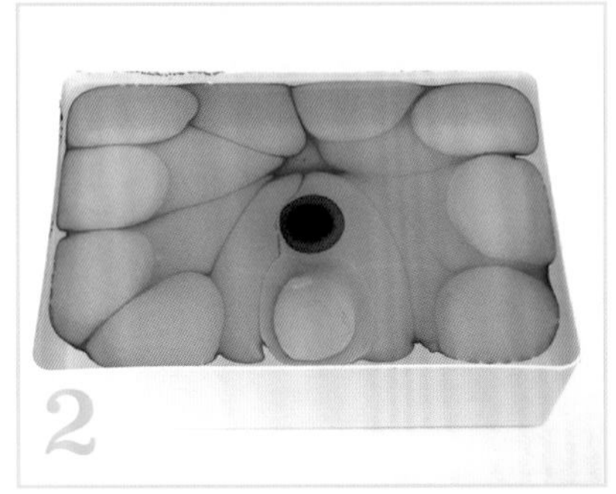

Drop a single drop at a time in the centre of the tray.

Wait for the drop to open.

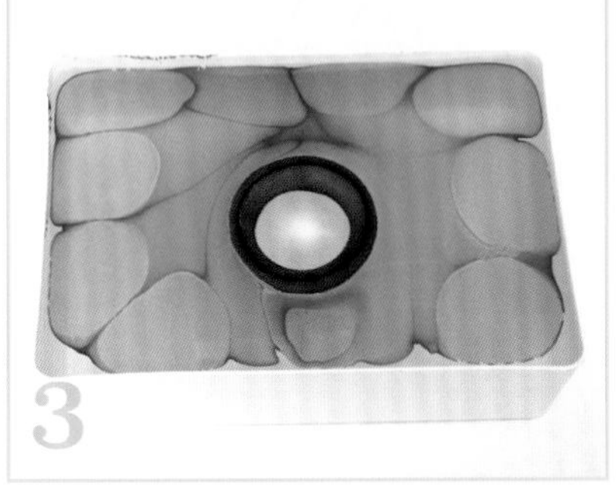

Repeat until you have 5 to 9 circles.

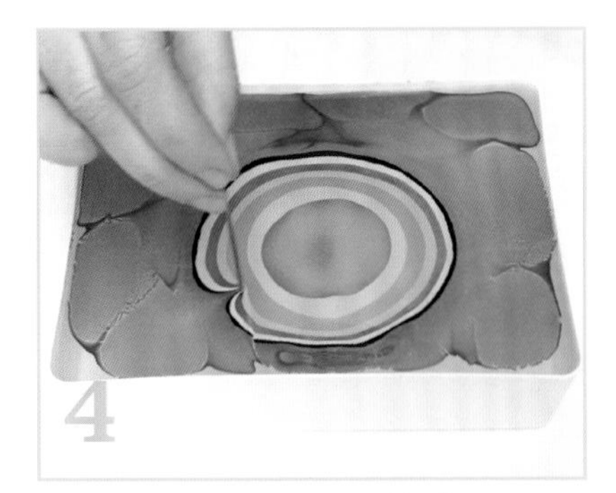

Using a stylus, pull the paint from the outside of the circle to the centre of the circle. Lift up your hand.

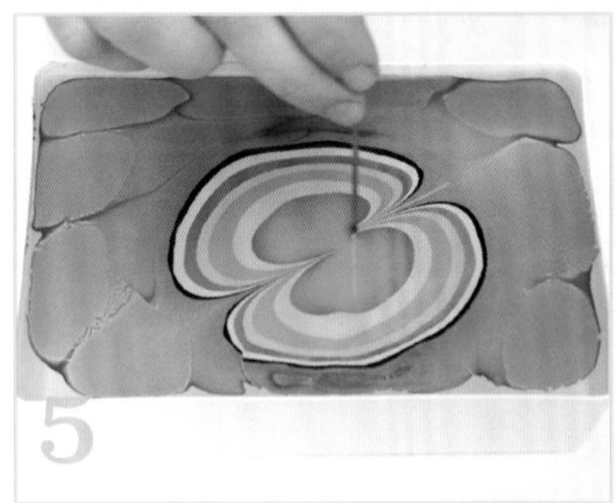

Do the same on the opposite side.

Repeat until you have as many petals as desired. Print.

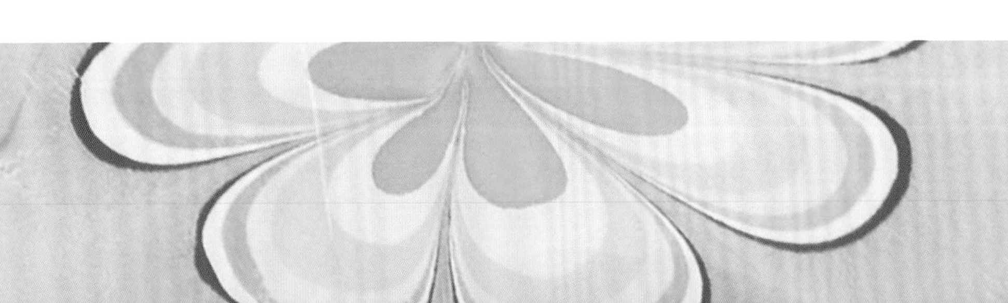

Four flower design

This is similar to the 'flower design' discussed previously, but done in the four corners of the tray.

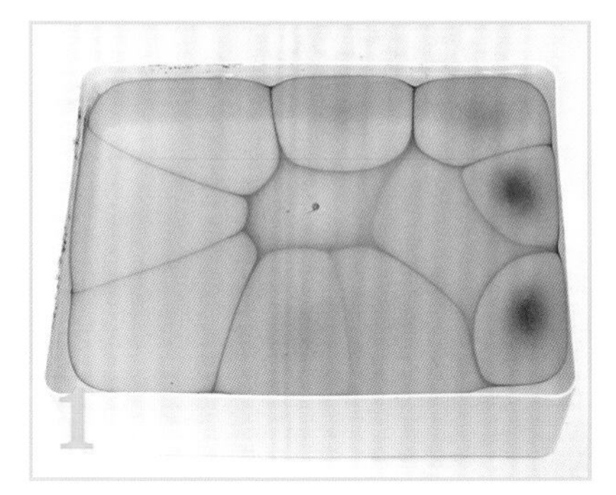

Start with a background colour. Wait for the drops to open up.

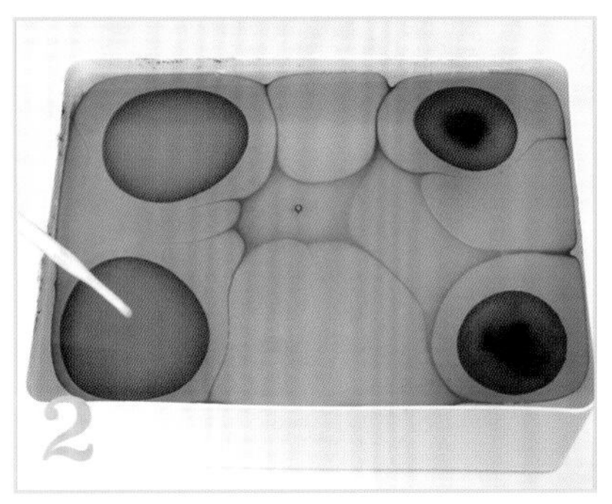

Place a drop just off each corner. Wait for the drops to open.

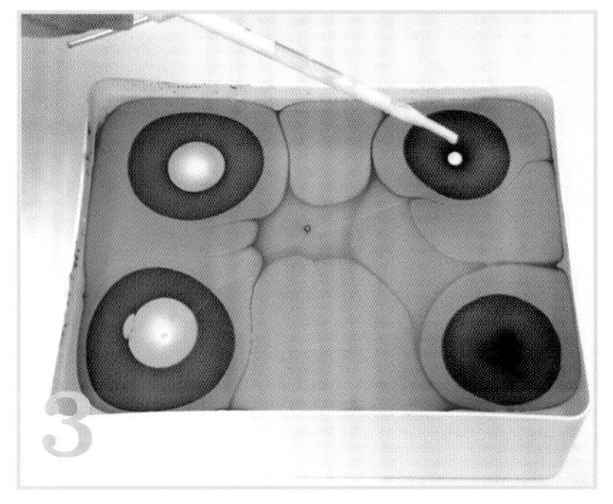

Drop the next drop of paint in the centre of each circle.

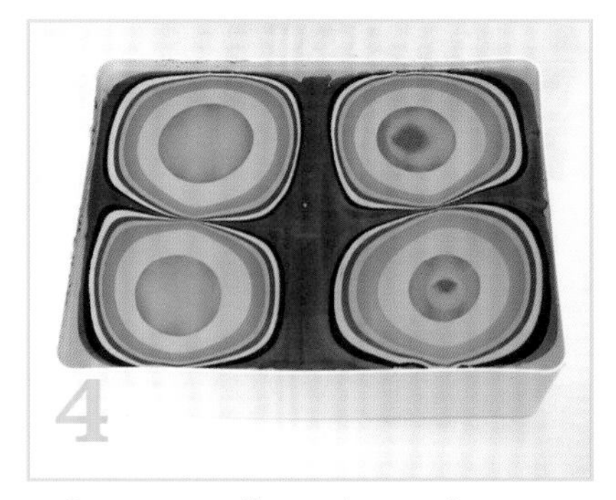

Repeat until you have about 4-5 circles.

Starting with one circle, create petals.

A little spiral can be created in the centre of each flower.

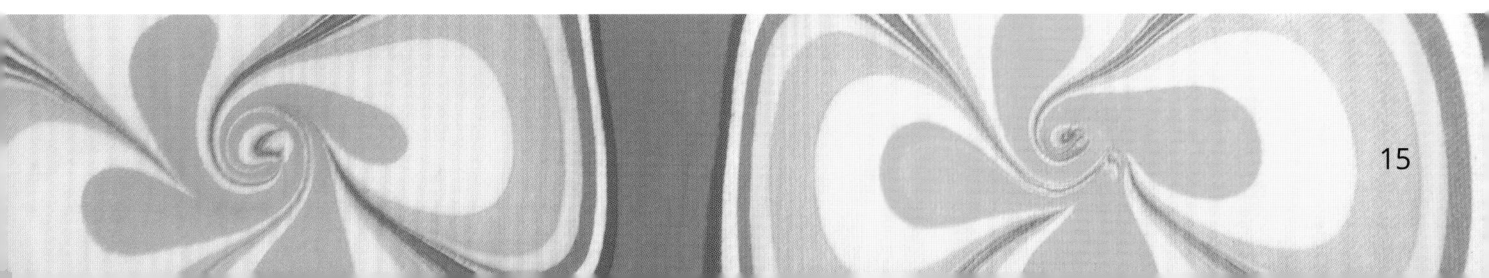

Heart design

This is similar to the 'four flower design' discussed previously.

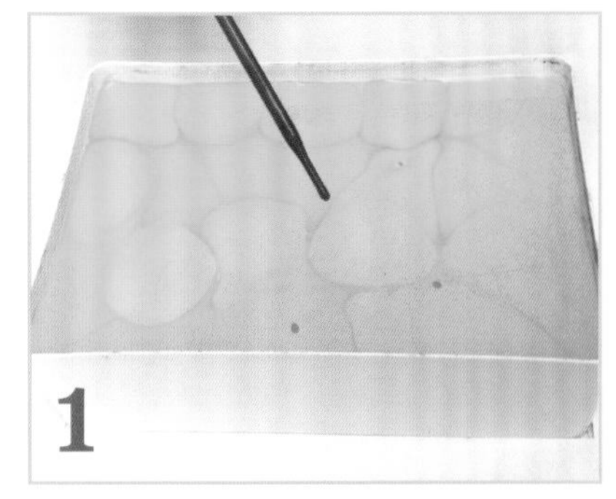

Start with a background colour. Wait for the drops to open up.

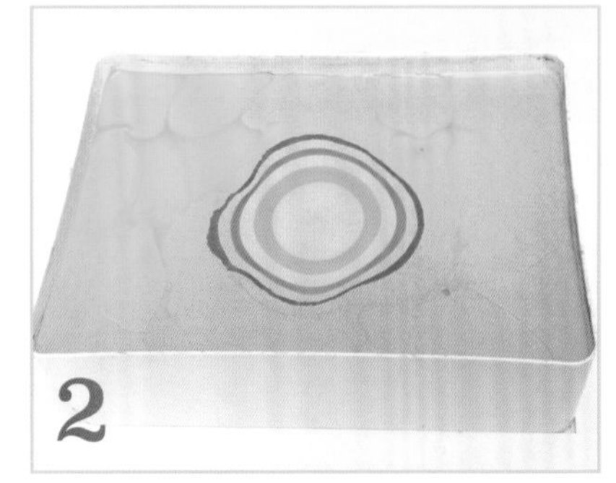

Place one drop at a time in the centre of the tray. Wait for the drop to open.

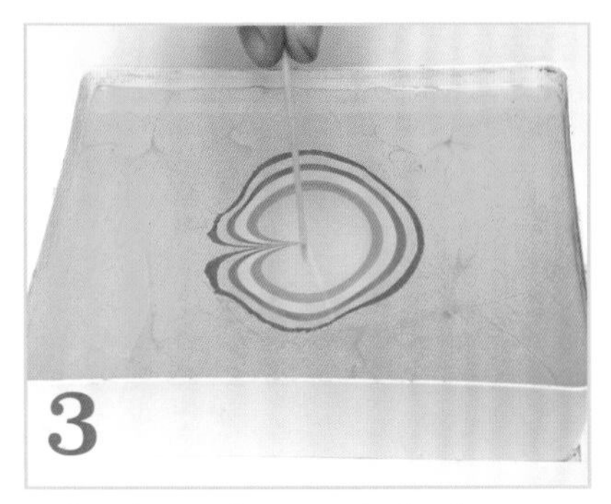

Cut through your circle, from one side...

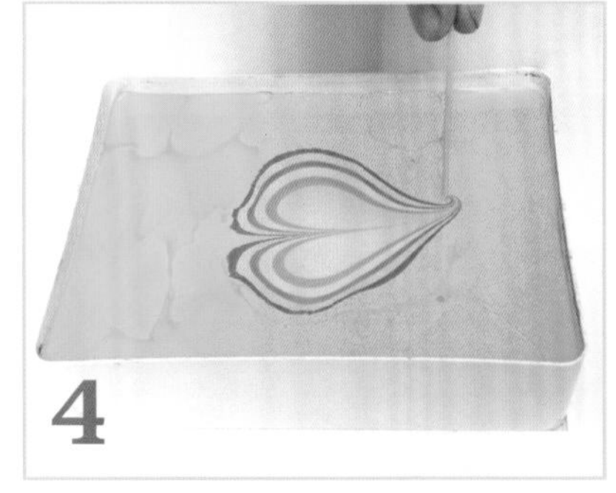

...to the other.

5 Print as previously described.

Four heart design

This design is a combination between the four flower and the heart design.

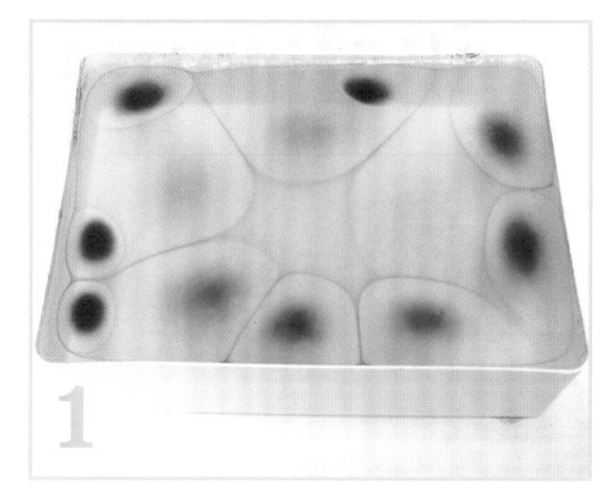

Start with a background colour. Wait for the drops to open up.

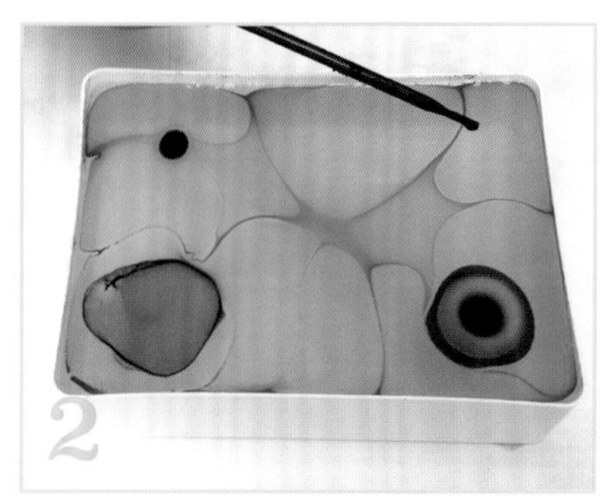

Place a drop just off each corner. Wait for the drops to open.

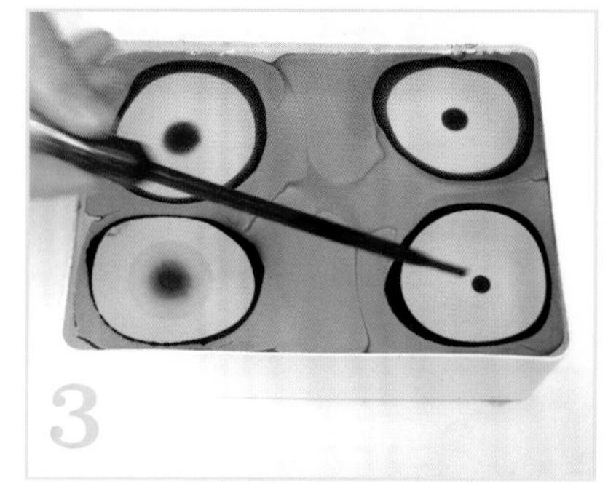

Drop the next colour of paint in the centre of each circle. Repeat until you have about 5 to 9 circles.

Starting from the corner of the tray, cut through the circle, stopping in the centre of the tray.

Repeat with the other circles.

Twirl in the centre to bring all four hearts together.

Freestyle

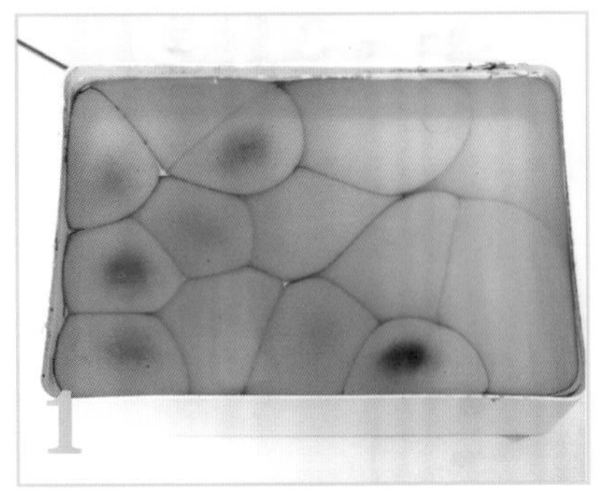

Start with a foundation colour.

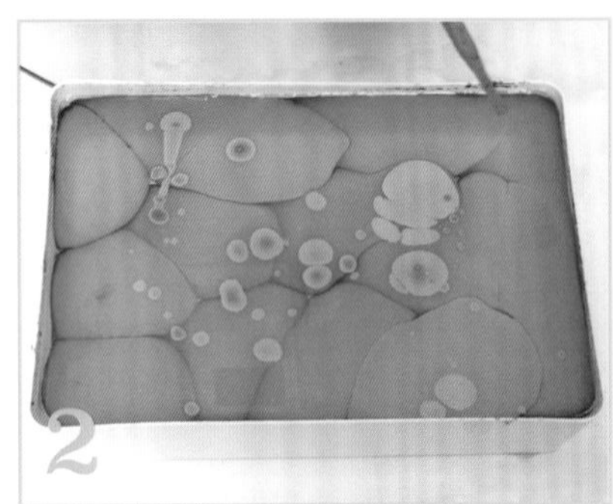

Stipple a contrasting colour over the background. Tap pipette on index finger for small drops.

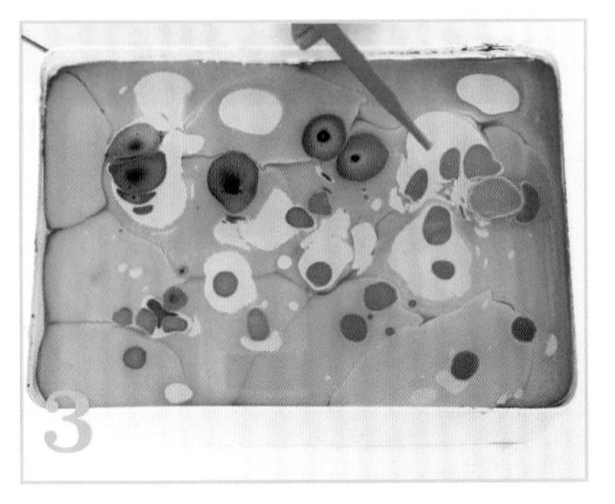

Continue to stipple different colours.

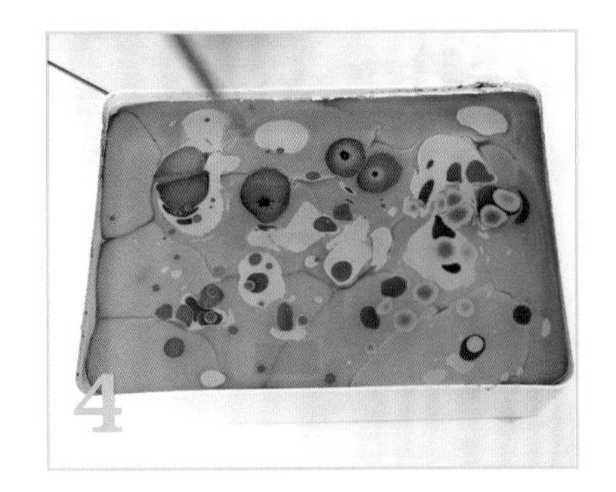

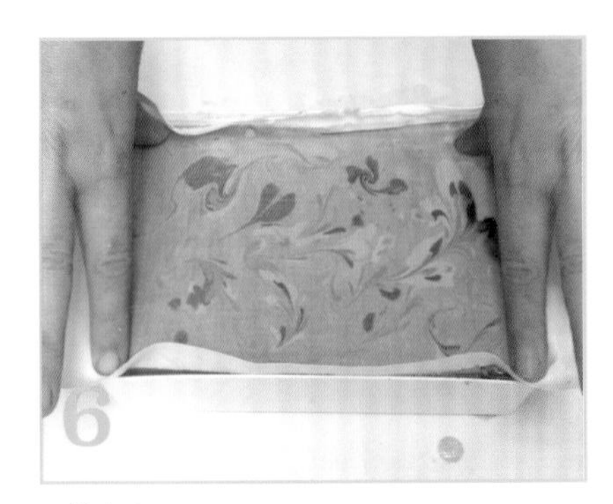

Add as many spirals or swirls as desired. It is possible to create mini flowers and hearts.

Print.

Chrysanthemum

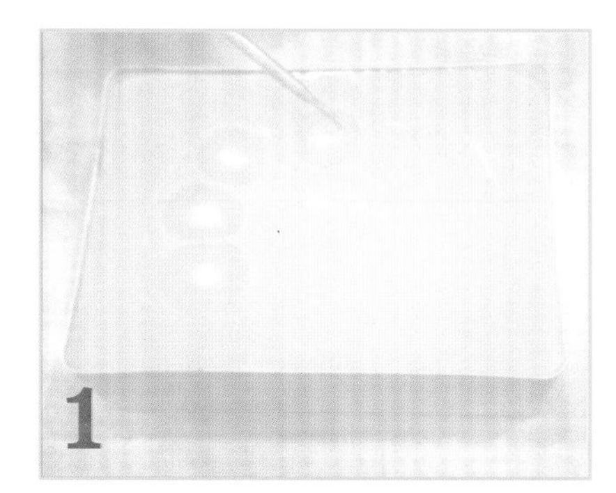

Start with a background colour. (White in this example).

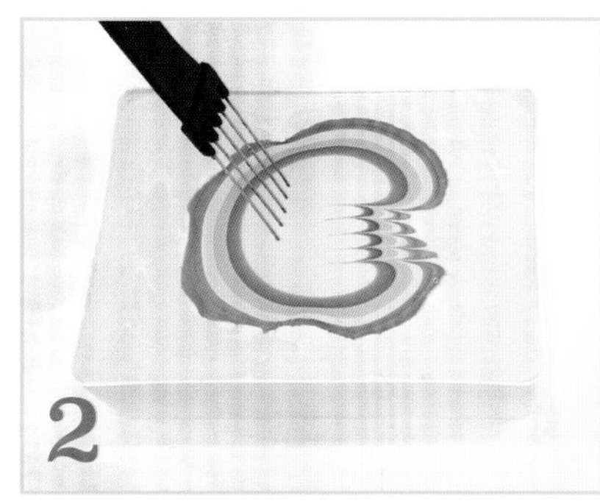

Start with creating a circle of about 6 layers. Use a comb to move to the centre of the circle by *just touching the very surface of the paint.*

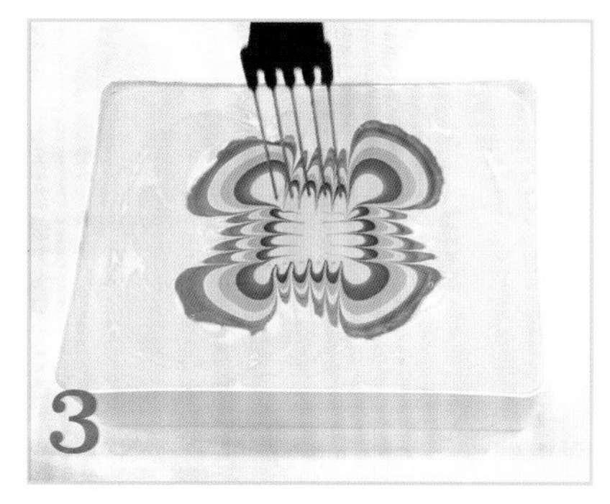

Use a comb and move the paint to the centre of the circle. Repeat this in opposite directions.

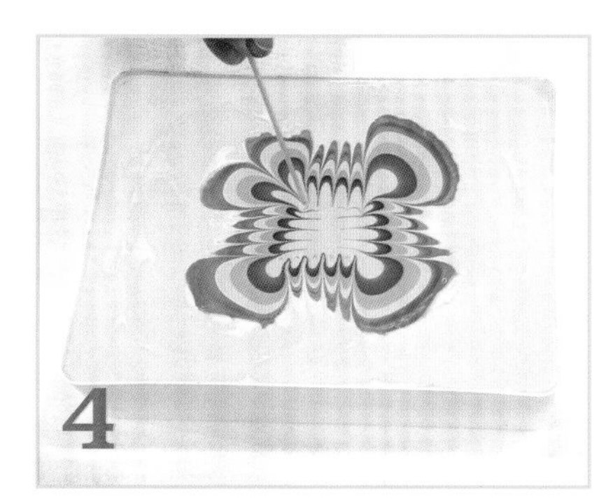

With a stylus, create more petals in the four corners,moving from the outside inwards.

If desired, create swirls by dragging paint from the inside, out and spiral.

Print.

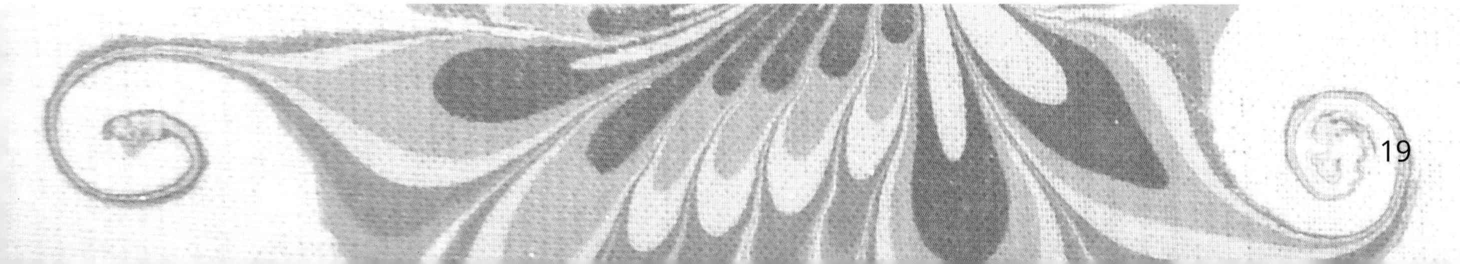

Starflower

Start with a background colour. Put one drop of paint in the centre of the tray. Wait for each drop to open before the next colour is released.

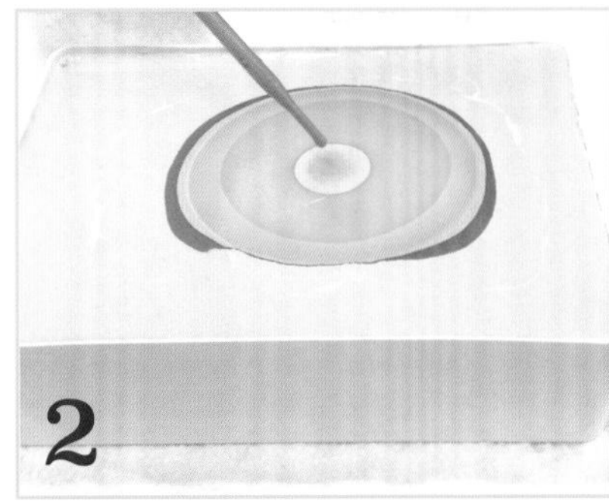

Continue until you have between 5 to 8 colours in the circle.

Drag the paint outwards with your stylus.

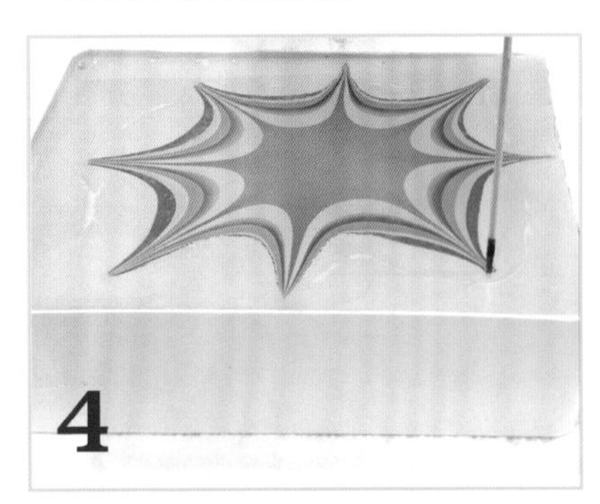

Continue until you have as many petals as desired, similar to a spider's web.

Pull the paint from the exterior (in between the web) to the centre. Spiral the centre.

Ghost

This is what is left on the surface after paper was printed.

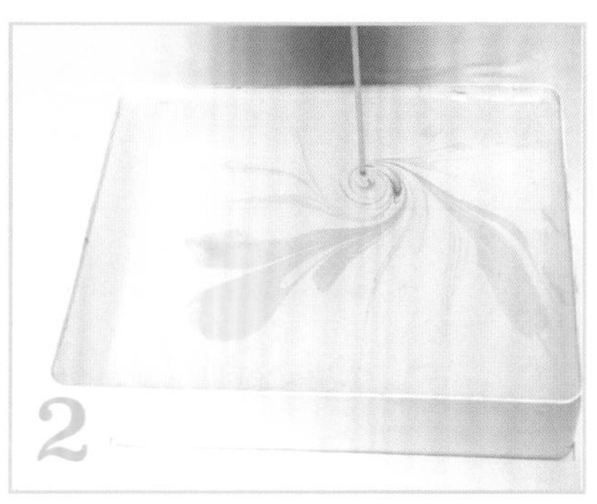

Adjust the design if desired.

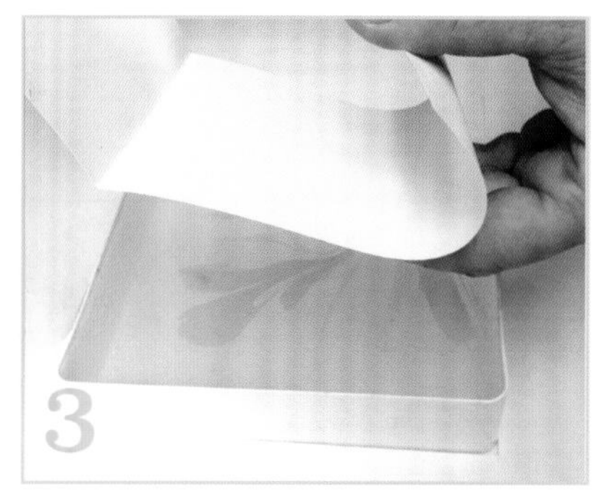

Slightly curl the paper before printing.

Roll the paper onto the design. (To avoid air pockets).

And lift off.

Leave to drip dry.

Stencil

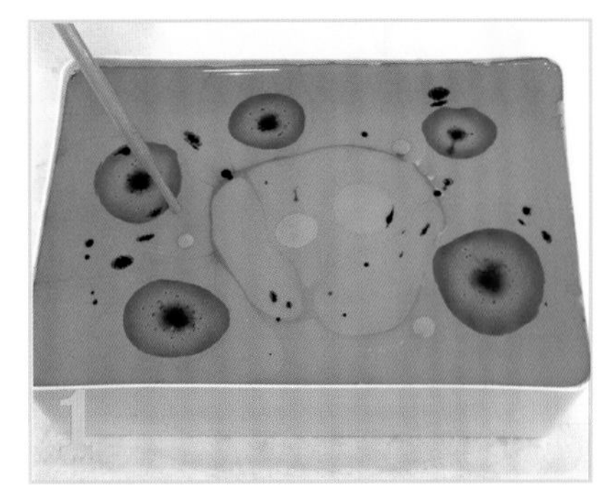

After the background colour, randomly place small drops of paint.

Create any intricate design. (In this case a chevron was created. See p. 27)

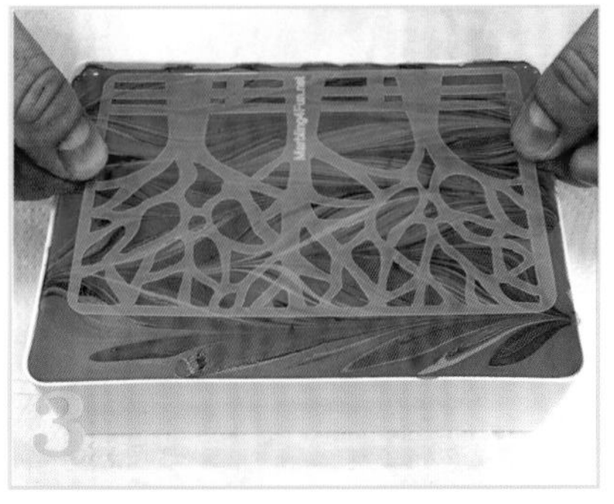

Carefully place a stencil on top of the design.

The stencil will float.

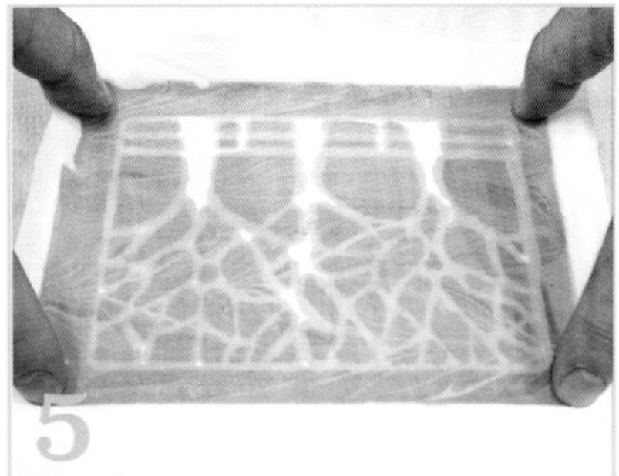

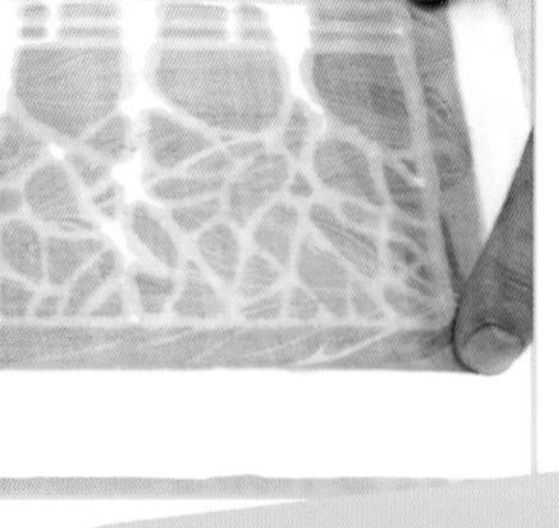

Print.

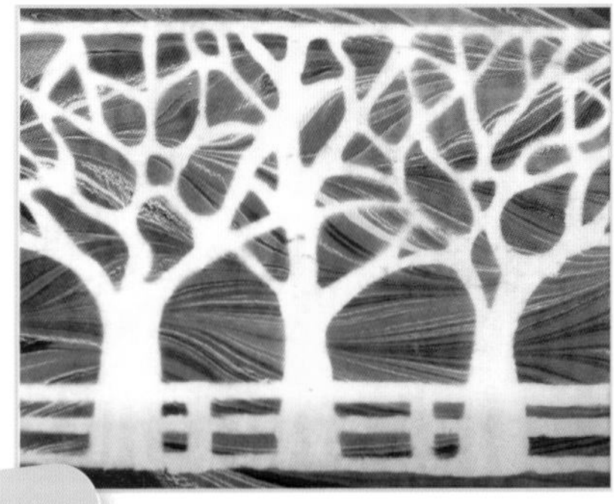

Most plastic stencils will work well.

There are stencils available www.marbling4fun.net/supplies

Christmas Tree

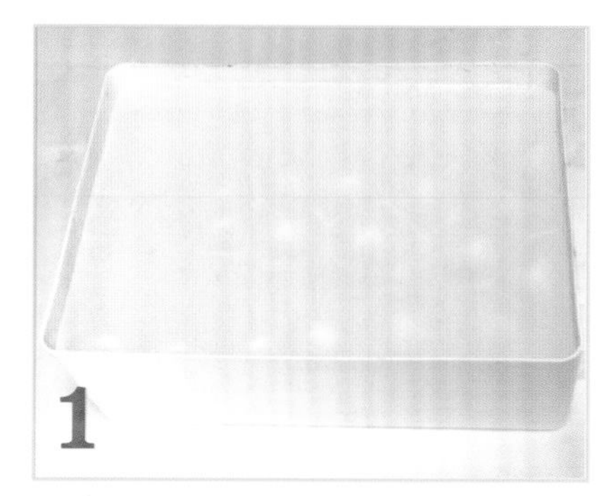
1

This was started with a white background colour.

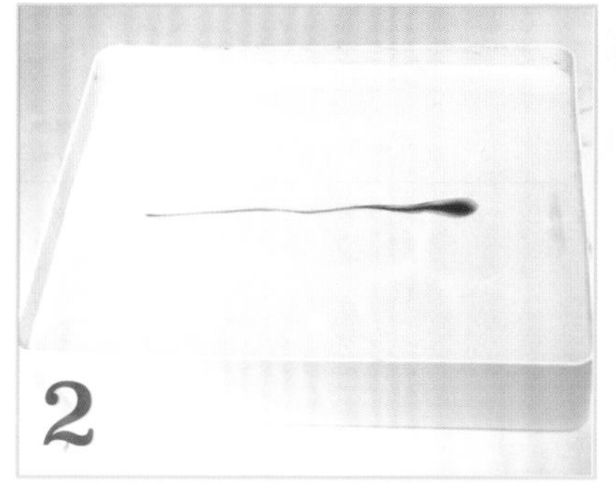
2

Drag a line with the pipette touching the very surface of the floater. No need to pinch the pipette.
Wait for the line to open.

3

Zig-zag through the line. A larger movement is needed for the trunk.

4

Pull a line through the zig-zag from bottom to top.

5

Place very small drops of paint around the tree. To make small drops: Dip the stylus in the paint and gently touch the floater surface.

6

Cut through the circles to make hearts.

Friendly Sharks

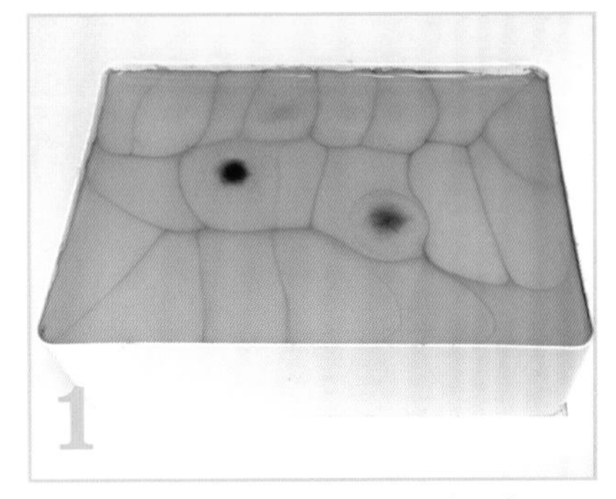

Start with a background colour of choice. Place two drops diagonally on the floater. Wait for them to open.

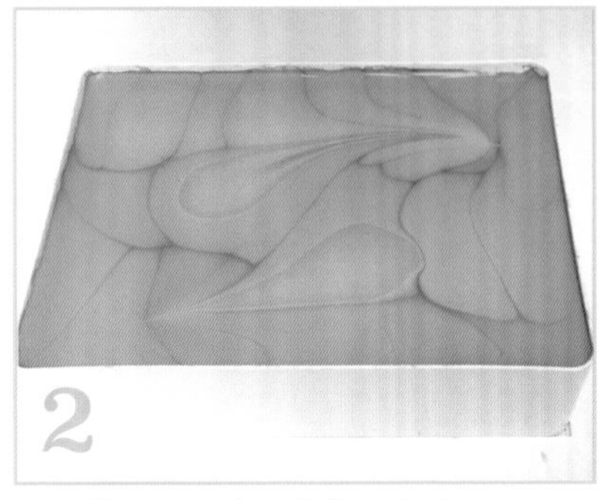

Pull one side of the circle outwards.

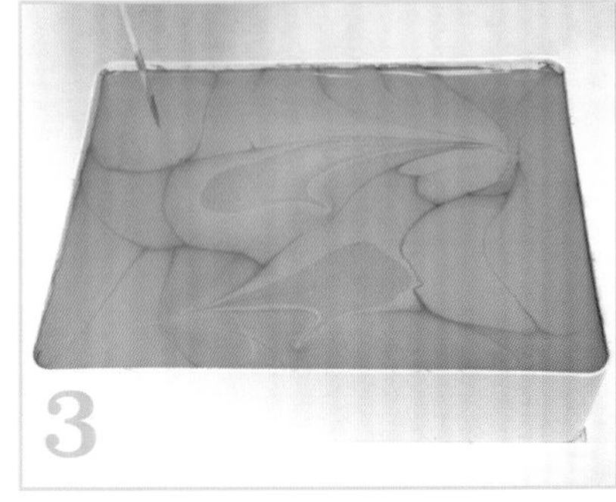

Make a little 'flick' upwards to create a fin.

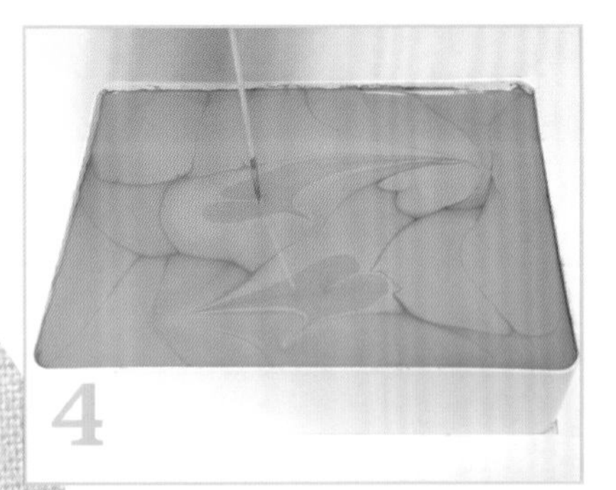

Pull the rounded curve inwards. This is to create the mouth.

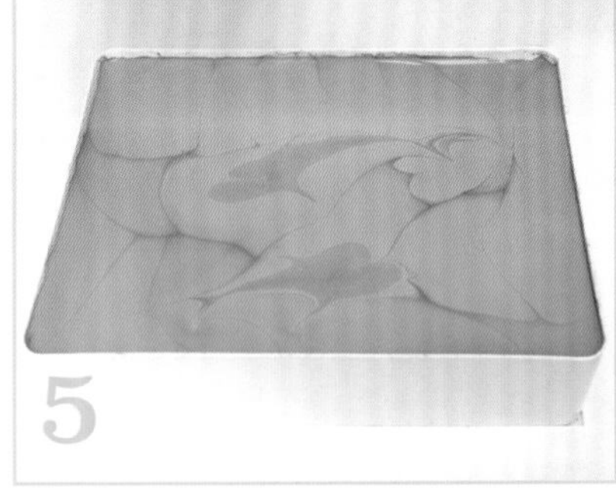

Gently move the paint at the pointed end outwards to create a tail. For the eye: Dip the stylus in paint and touch the surface of the floater.

Birds

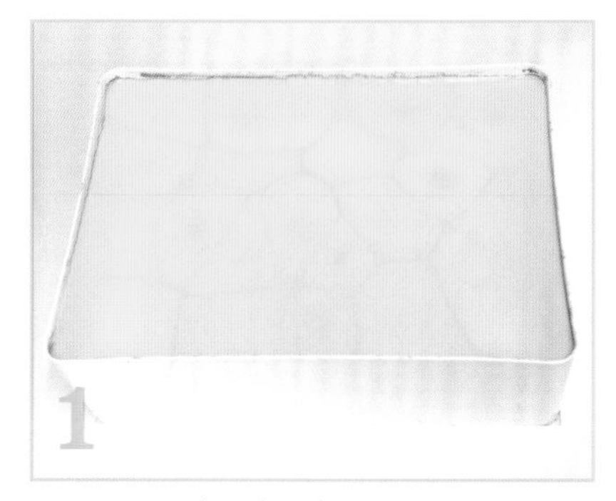

Start with a background colour of choice.

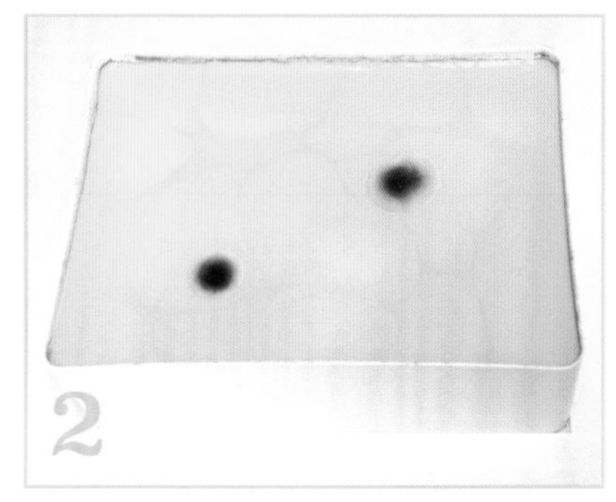

Place 2 drops diagonally on the floater surface. Wait for the drops to open.

Create hearts. From the edge of the tray inwards. (You have now created space for the body and wings).

For the wings: With a stylus, pull three lines of paint outwards .

For the beak: On the curved side, pull the paint outwards. For the eye: touch the floater with the stylus dipped in paint.

Traditional designs

Stone Marble (Turkish Marble)

! Top Tips *Do not over do the veins. They will become compact and fabric/paper will be unable to absorb all the paint and as a result smudge.*

For Gold Vein Marble, start the base colour with gold paint, available at www.marbling4fun.net/supplies

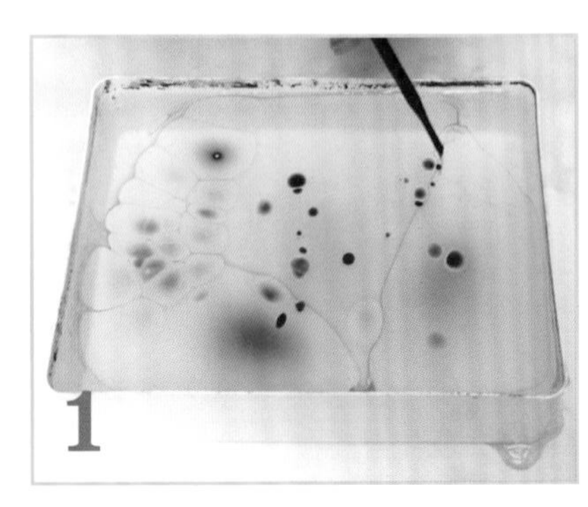

Stipple paint onto the surface of the floater.

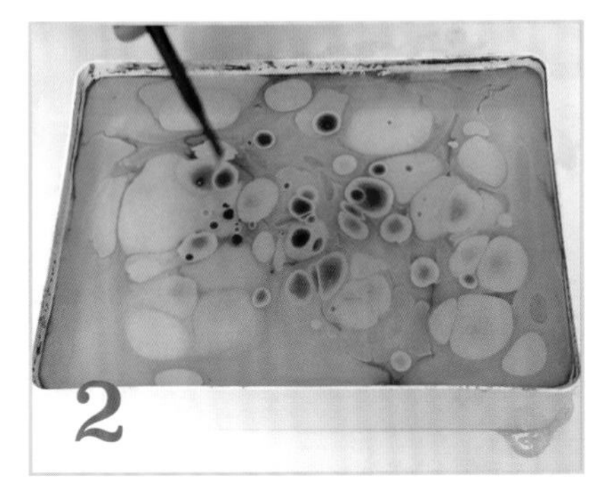

Stipple another colour onto the surface of the first. Continue until you have created veins. Print without manipulating the design.

Gold Vein

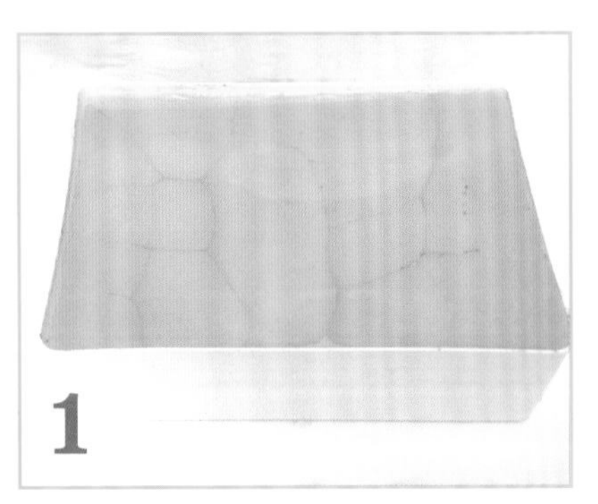

Stipple paint onto the surface of the floater.

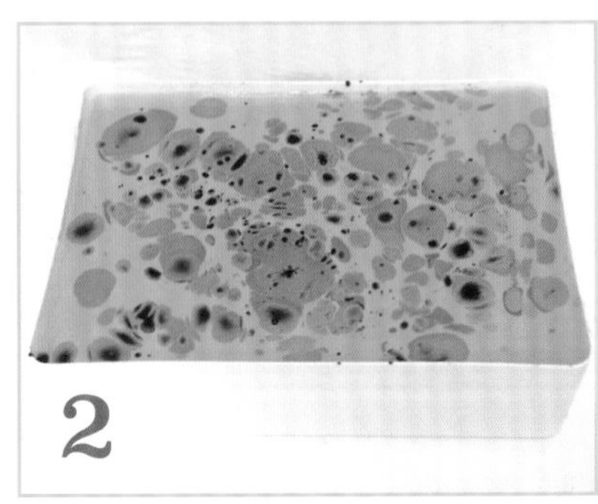

Stipple another colour onto the surface of the first. The paint will find its own space.

Chevron

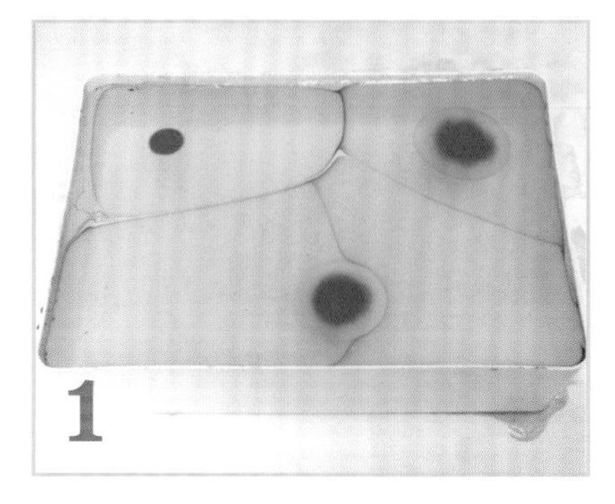

Randomly place your colours in the tray.

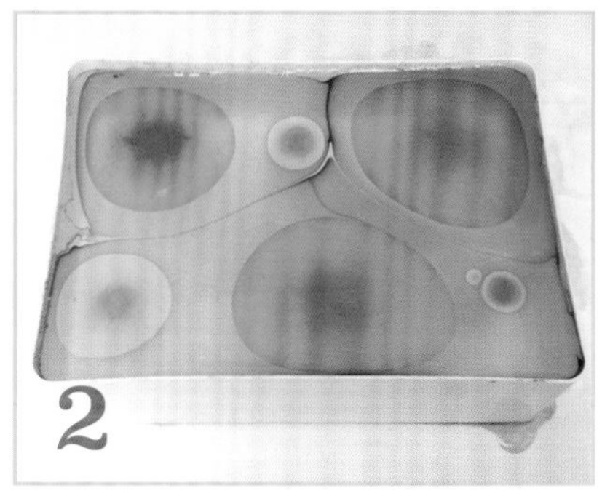

Randomly place contrasting colours in the tray.

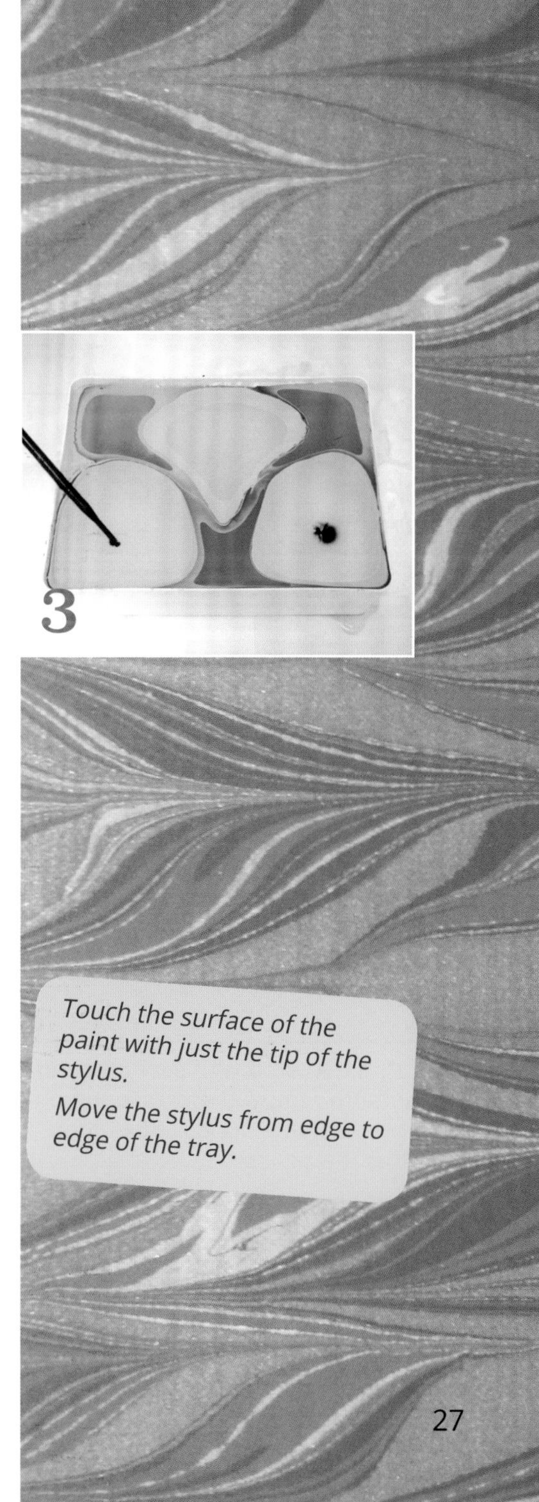

Touch the surface of the paint with just the tip of the stylus.

Move the stylus from edge to edge of the tray.

Zig-zag in parallel lines from one side to the other.

Zig-zag in parallel lines across the previous lines

Arch Marble

The teeth of the comb should be about 2cm apart.

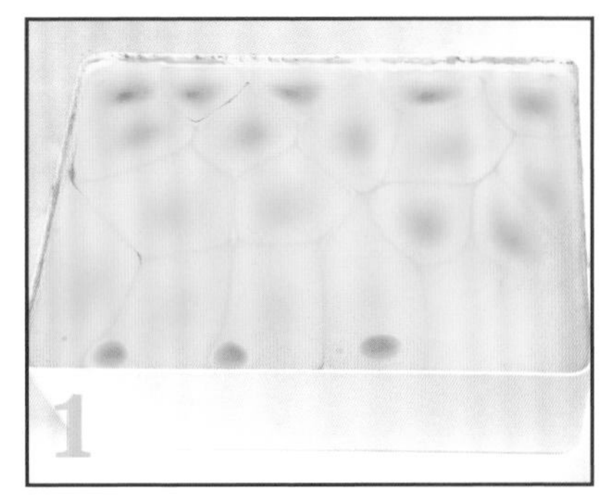

Start with a background colour.

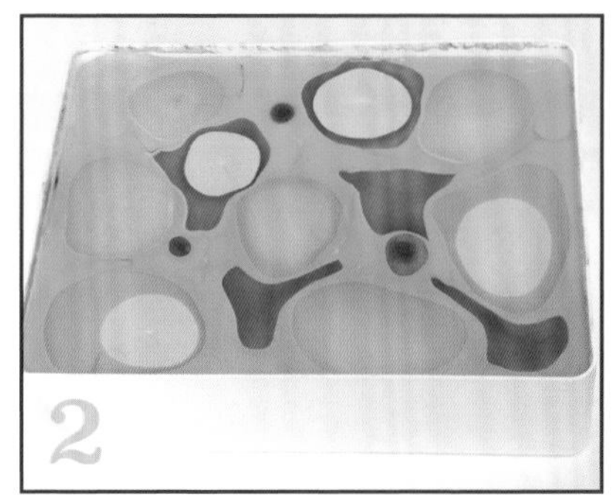

Place colours randomly over the surface.

Using a stylus or toothpick, create zig-zags.

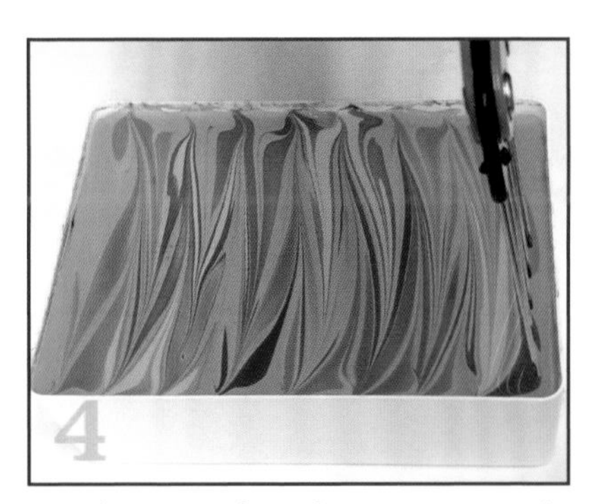

Take a comb with every second tooth removed and rake the paint in the opposite direction as the zig- zag.

Touch only the very surface of the paint else too much paint will be dragged along.

Leather pouch

Nonpareil marble

This is the same as Arch Marble, but the spacing between the teeth of the comb is reduced to about 0.5cm.

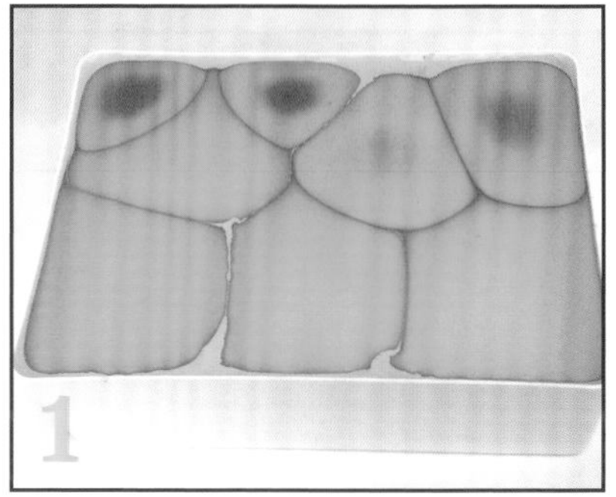

Start with placing colours randomly over the surface.

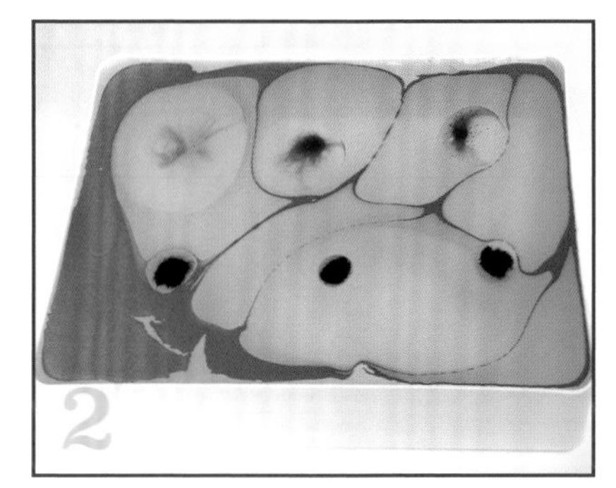

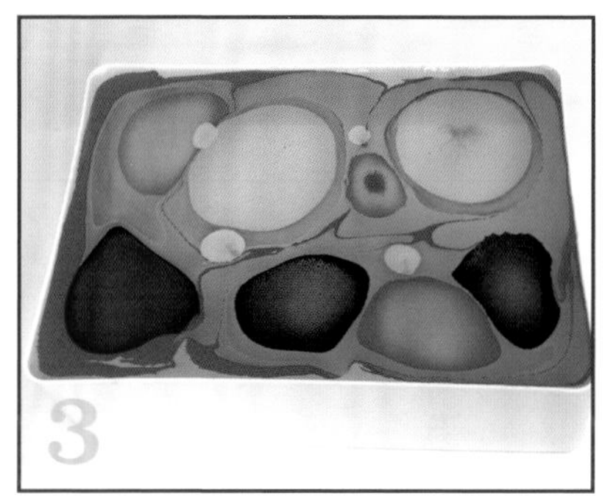

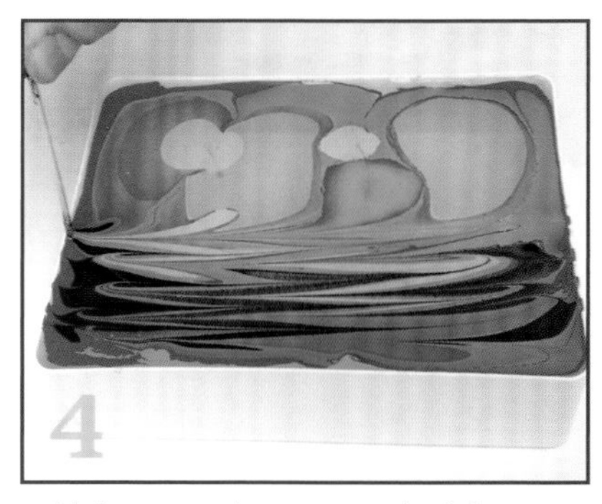

Using a stylus or toothpick, move through the paint in a zig-zag movement.

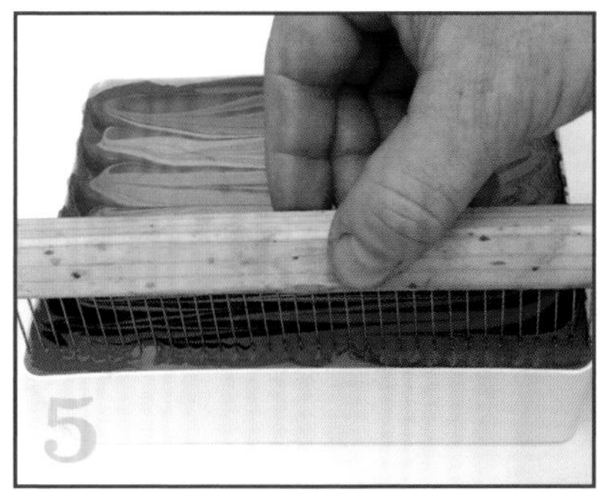

Take care to touch the very surface of the paint.

Take a comb and rake the paint in the opposite direction as the zig-zag.
Extra care should be taken when raking the paint with the comb.
As the teeth are about 5mm apart, a slow movement is needed.

A comb with pins was used as pins are fine. This will drag less paint.

Fountain

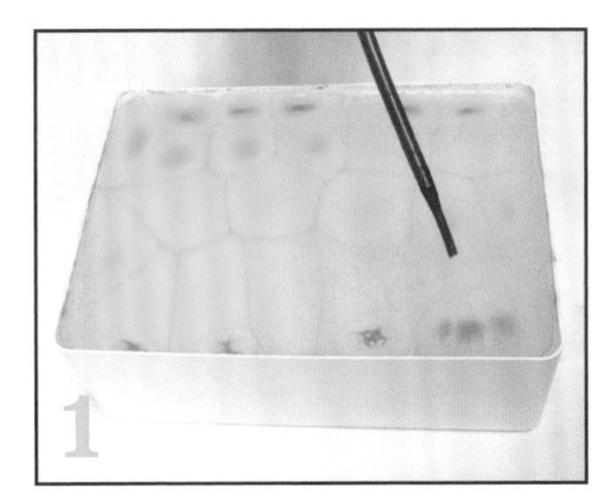

Start with a background colour.

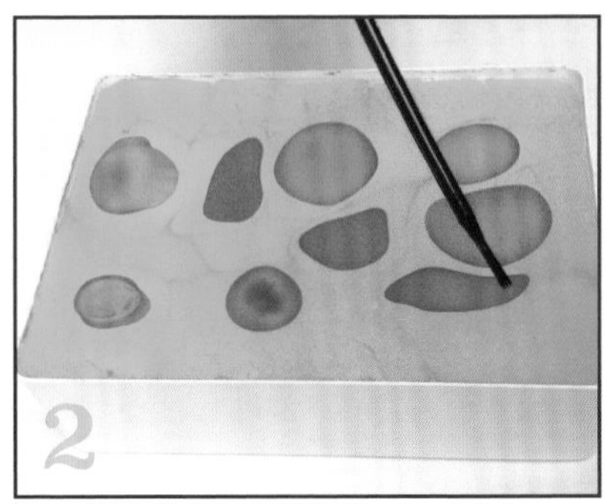

Randomly place colours on the surface.

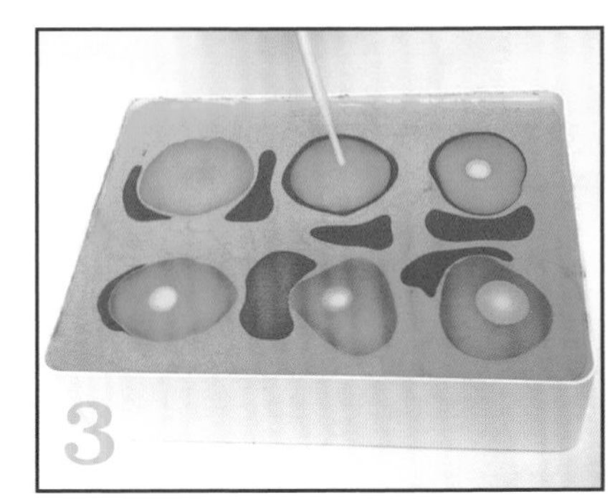

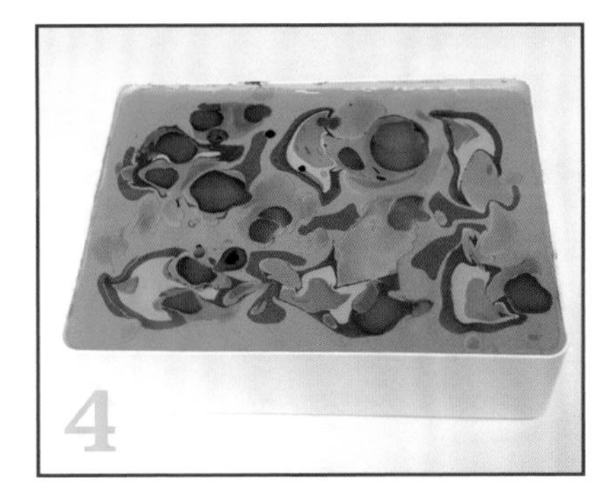

Rake the paint with a comb with teeth set at about 2cm apart.

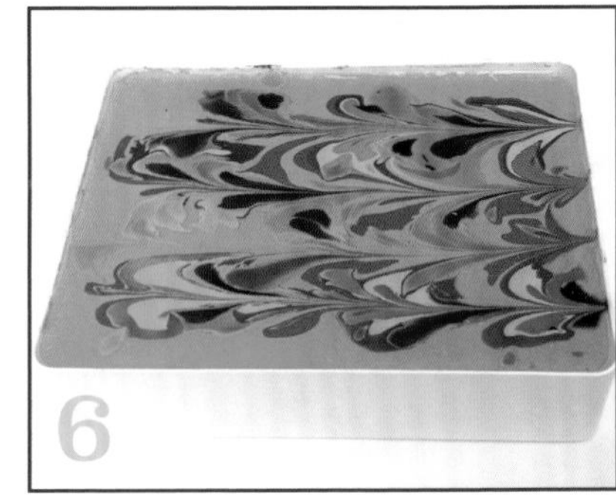

Print

American

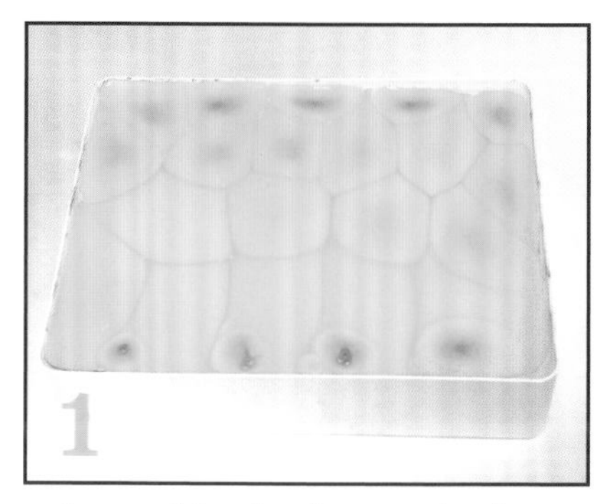

Start with a background colour.

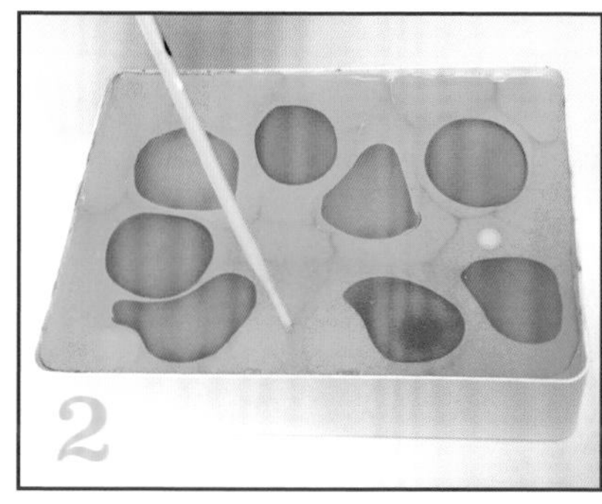

Randomly place your colours.

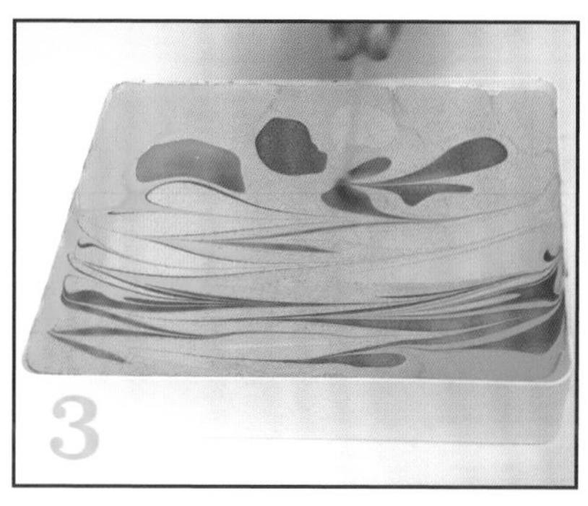

Create zig-zag lines.

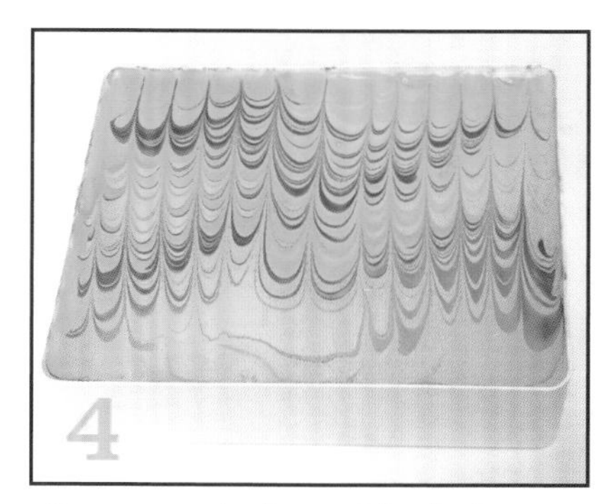

Create an Arch marble design (p.28)

With the same comb, move in the opposite direction as the lines of the Arch marble design.

Spanish marble

This design works best on paper.

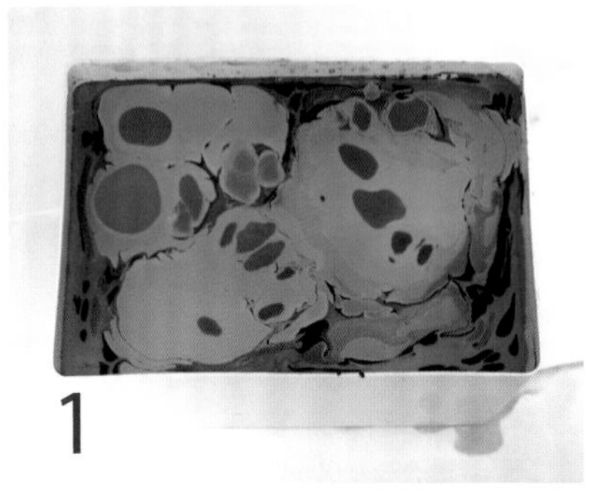

Start with a stone marble design.
Slightly curl the paper which is about to be printed.

When laying the paper down, start from one end and gently move the paper forward and backwards.

Lowering it slightly more each time.
Lift off the floater, gently rinse and hang to dry.

This is the only design that is not printed in one continuous movement. The paper has to be moved forwards and backwards as it is lowered.

Italian

Tip: Pinch the skin of an orange peel above the design for the white-out spots

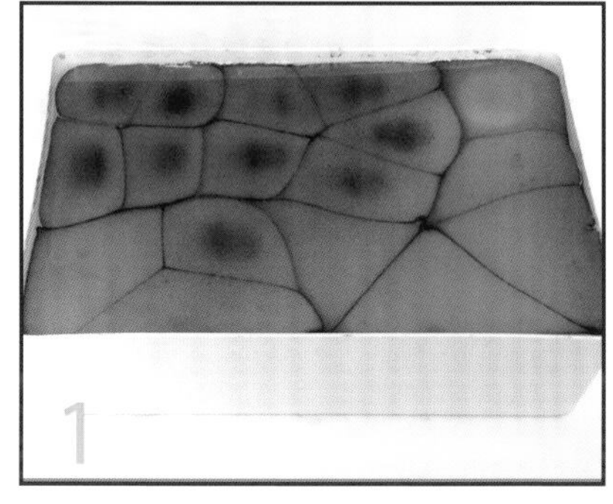

Start with a background colour.

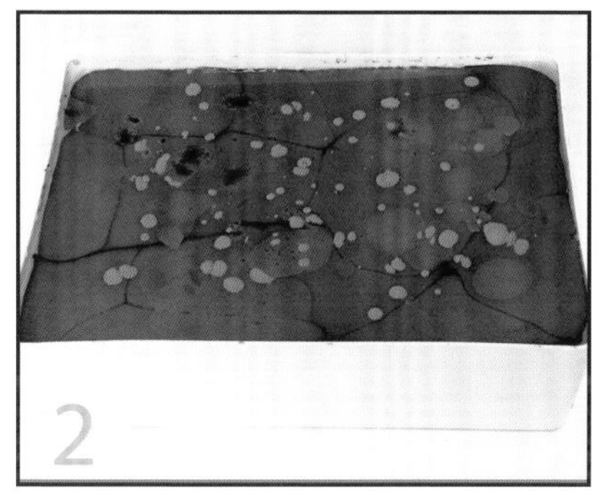

Create a Stone marble design. (See p.26)

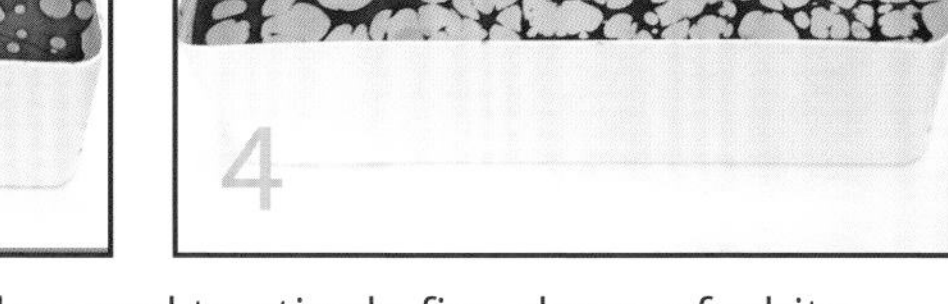

A clean old toothbrush can be used to stipple fine drops of white paint. Run your fingers over the bristles.

Alternatively, squeeze the outside peel of an orange or clementine in *the air above* the design, not directly pointing to the design.

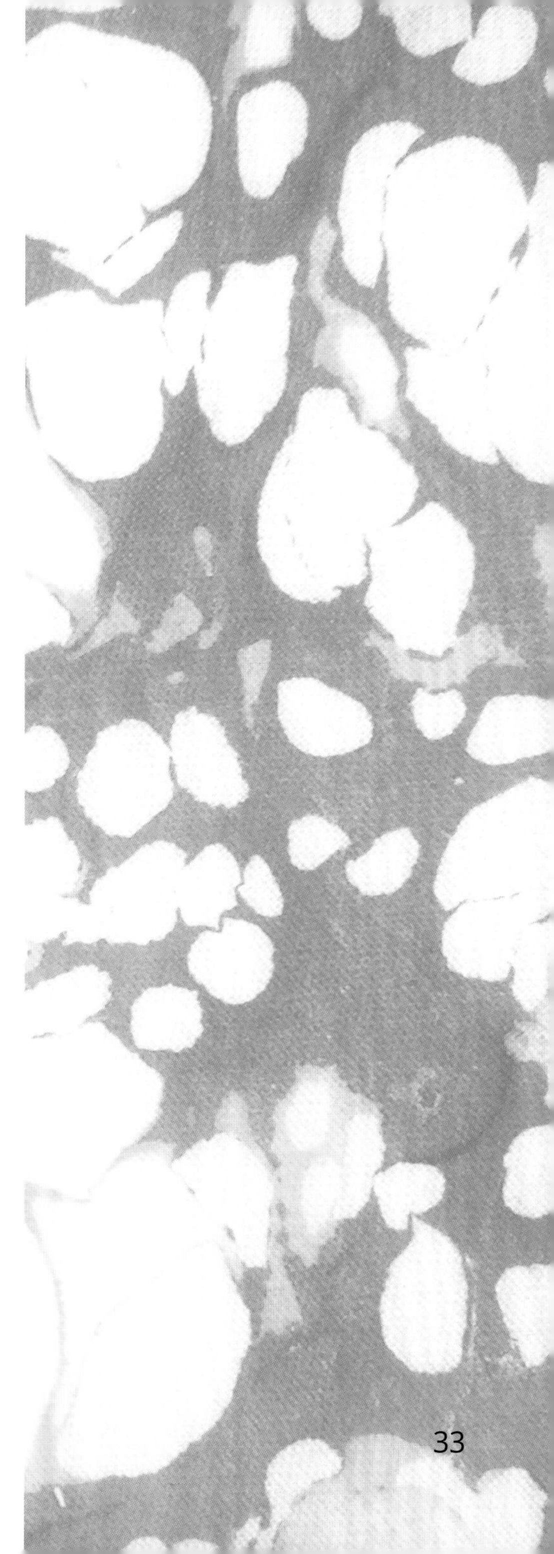

Zebra marble

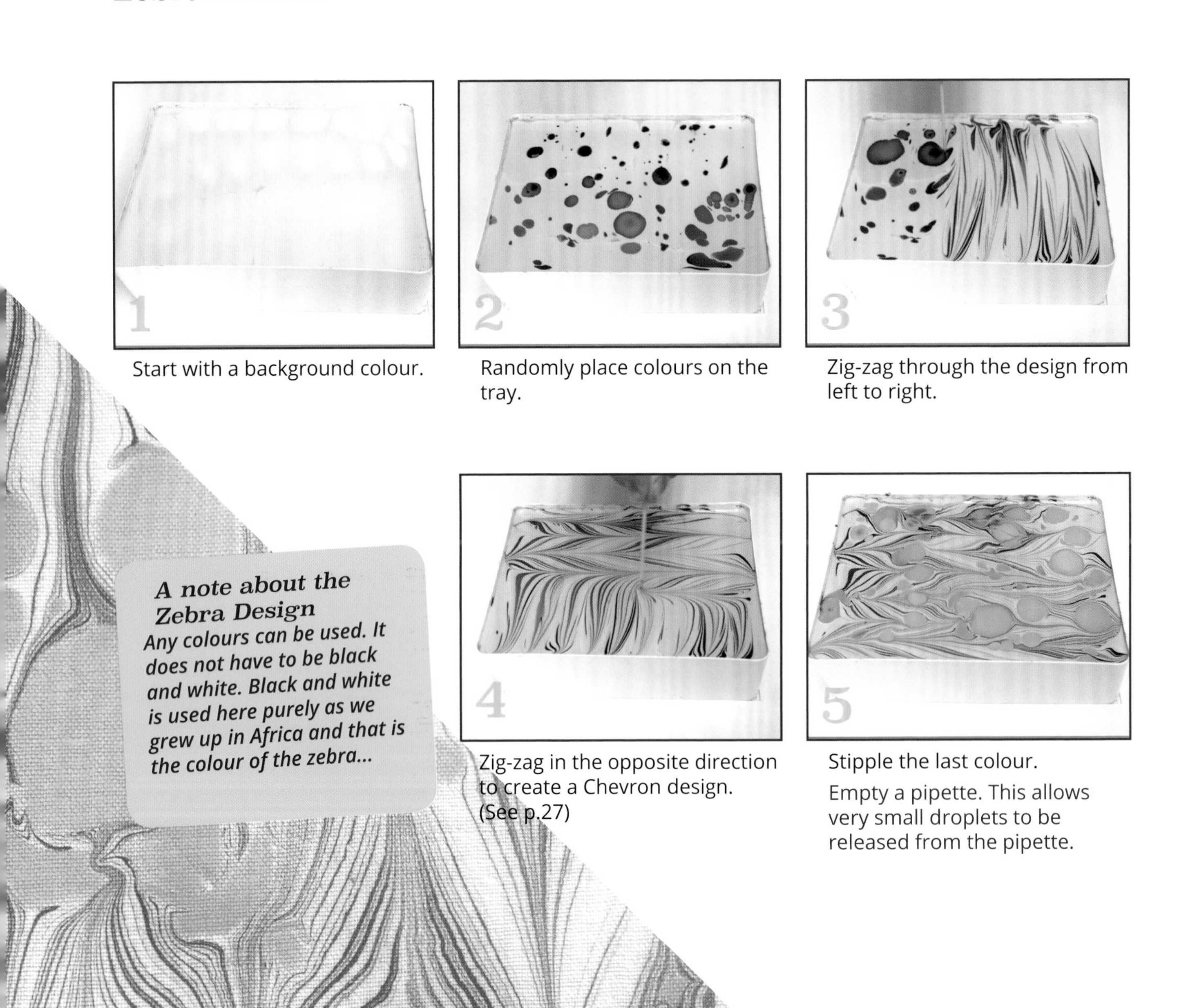

Start with a background colour.

Randomly place colours on the tray.

Zig-zag through the design from left to right.

Zig-zag in the opposite direction to create a Chevron design. (See p.27)

Stipple the last colour.

Empty a pipette. This allows very small droplets to be released from the pipette.

A note about the Zebra Design

Any colours can be used. It does not have to be black and white. Black and white is used here purely as we grew up in Africa and that is the colour of the zebra...

Snail marble/ French curl

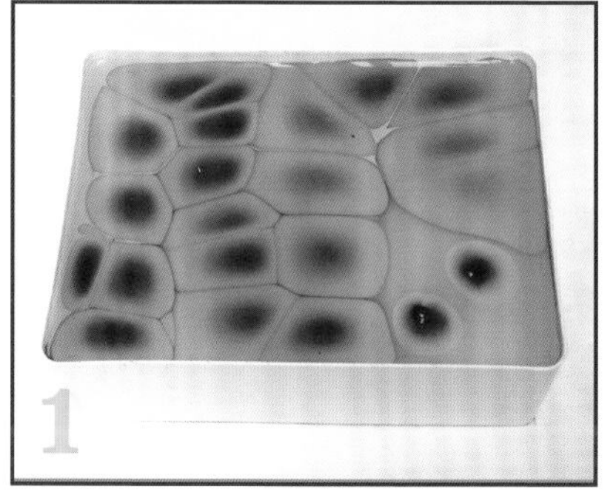

Start with a Stone marble.
(See p.26)

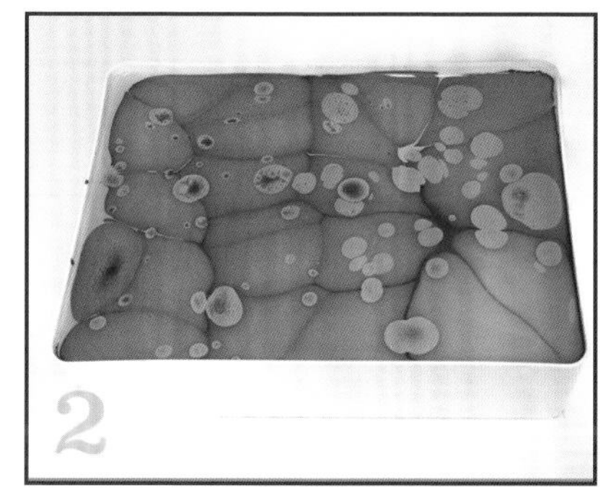

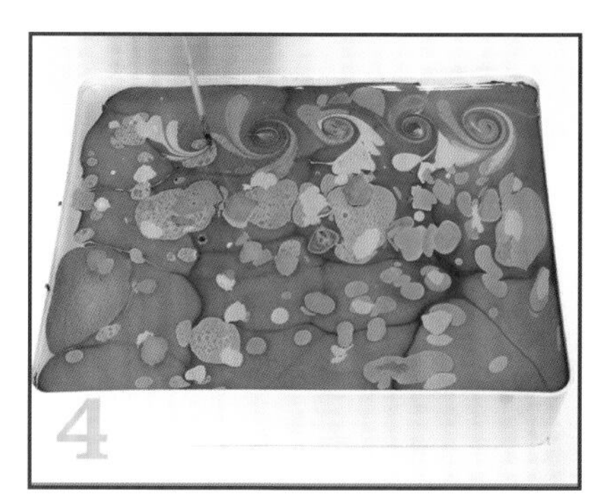

Use a stylus to create spirals.
Keep the spirals equidistant and in the same direction.

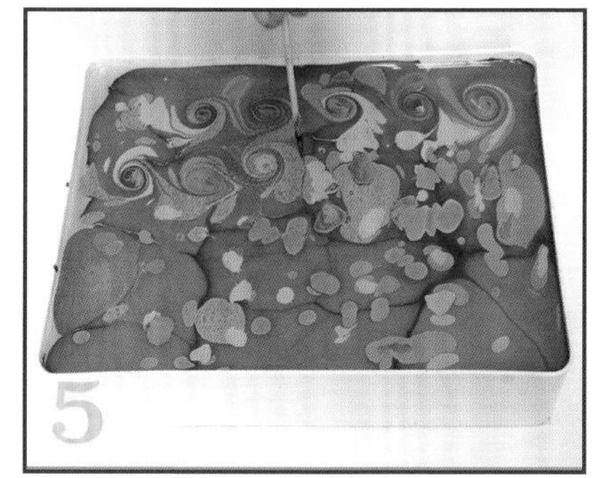

Print.

The spirals move from the inside out.

Keep the spirals equal distance from each other.

Double Print

To add further detail to a previous print, make it a double print.

Choose a design created previously.

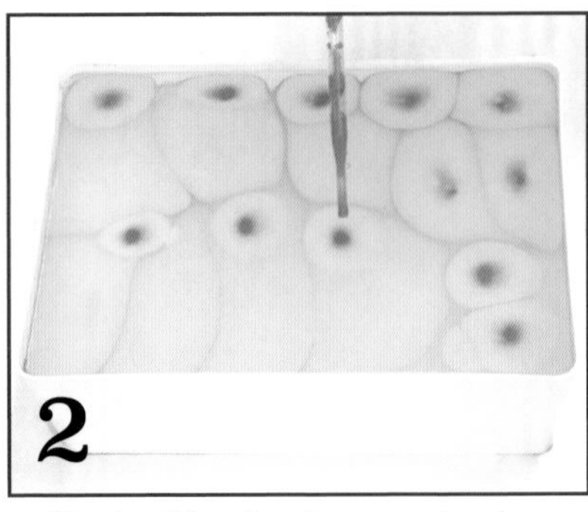

Start with a background colour.

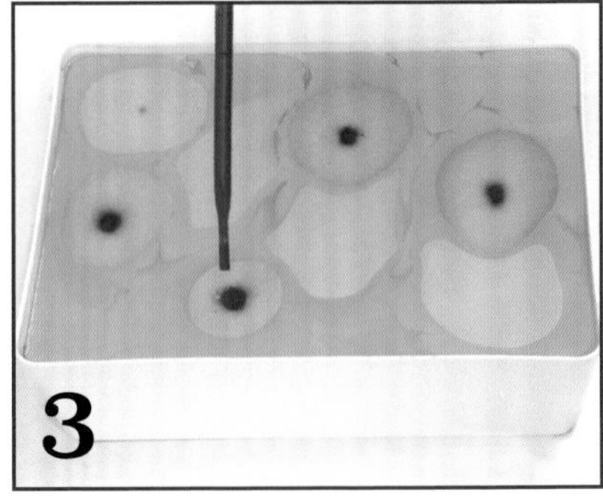

Create any design you desire.

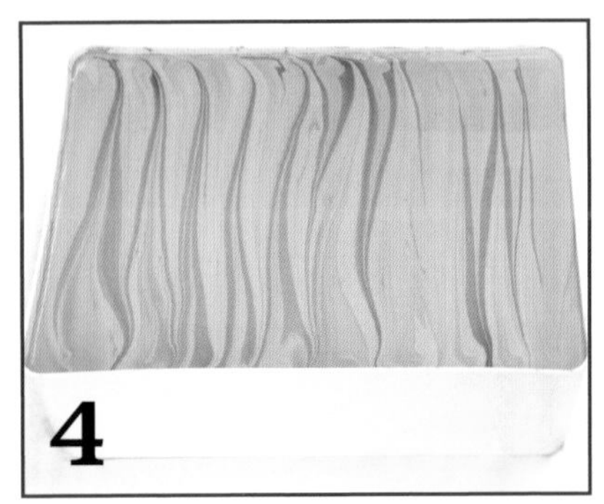

In this print: Create lines

Zig-zag across the lines.

Print over the first design. The paint is transparent, therefore you can see through the original design.